UNEXPECTED FREEDOM

Discover Peace and Joy in the Reality of Life

TARA LALONDE

Foreword by Kary Oberbrunner

Author of ELIXER Project, *Day Job to Dream Job*,
The Deeper Path, and *Your Secret Name*

Published by Author Academy Elite
PO Box 43, Powell, OH, 43035
www.AuthorAcademyElite.com

Library of Congress Control Number: 2016913304
Author Academy Elite, Powell, OH

ISBN-13: 978-1943526772
ISBN-10: 194352677X

"Who I Am in Christ" by Neil Anderson, *Victory Over the Darkness* Bethany House Publishers, a division of Baker Publishing Group, Copyright © August 2000, Used by permission.

"The Wonderful Cross," Chris Tomlin, J.D. Walt, Jesse Reeves, Copyright © 2000 worshiptogether.com Songs (ASCAP) sixsteps Music (ASCAP) Vamos Publishing (ASCAP) (adm. at CapitolCMGPublishing.com) All rights reserved. Used by permission.

Unless otherwise indicated, Scripture quotations are from The Holy Bible, New International Version®, NIV® Copyright © 1973, 1978, 1984, 2011 by Biblica, Inc.® Used by permission. All rights reserved worldwide.

Scripture quotations marked (NLT) are taken from the *Holy Bible*, New Living Translation, copyright © 1996, 2004, 2007, 2013 by Tyndale House Foundation. Used by permission of Tyndale House Publishers, Inc., Carol Stream, Illinois 60188. All rights reserved.

Scripture quotations marked (ESV) are taken from The Holy Bible, English Standard Version Copyright © 2001 by Crossway Bibles, a publishing ministry of Good News Publishers.

Scripture quotations marked (TLB) are taken from The Living Bible copyright © 1971 by Tyndale House Foundation. Used by permission of Tyndale House Publishers Inc., Carol Stream, Illinois 60188. All rights reserved.

The Internet addresses in this book are accurate at the time of publication. They are provided as a resource. Tara Lalonde or the publisher do not endorse them or vouch for their content or permanence.

Dedication

To those who have fearlessly traversed the valley of dying
to self before us and pointed the way, and to those
who will courageously take this journey.

Contents

Foreword

For over a decade Tara has been leading and encouraging her clients to face the hard things in their lives and find freedom, renewal, and hope. During that time she has also walked her own journey with God as He has continued to refine her and teach her how to walk ever closer with Him. In the process she has learned what it means to surrender to God in many things—a process she calls dying to self.

When we first talked about her writing this book her passion and enthusiasm to help others gain this incredible freedom was contagious. Her candid and yet gentle style allows her to speak difficult truths in a way that is both digestible and encouraging.

If you are tired of struggling through life and feeling like God is not interested in you, this is the book for you. Tara reveals false beliefs that set us up for missing what God truly has for us.

Her writing blends a mix of research, personal experience, and stories of others who have taken this journey and experienced the riches on the other side. Tara guides readers through the valley of dying to self to the other side where deep peace can be found regardless of the continued circumstances of life.

You will see that even though we are not always able to change our situations, we do not need to be overcome, discouraged, or defeated by them either. Through powerful changes in perspective you can find the surpassing peace and joy that the Apostle Paul talks about, even in the midst of your real life trials. Why not start your journey to freedom today?

Kary Oberbrunner
Author of *ELIXIR Project, Day Job to Dream Job, The Deeper Path,* and *Your Secret Name*

Introduction

O the wonderful cross,
Bids me come and die and find that I may truly live
...
Love so amazing, so divine
Demands my soul, my life, my all
ISAAC WATTS/CHRIS TOMLIN

As I stood in church this morning with hundreds of other believers singing this hymn, "O the Wonderful Cross," these two lines jumped off the screen once again. I had already begun the writing process, preparing for this book, but I had been struggling to find a way to introduce it. This hymn focused me on the crux of my message. I have been on a journey of learning what it is to "die" and "truly live" for so many years, that the experience is often hard to put into words. Singing these words propelled me into the exhilarating depths of my passion, which I long for you to experience as well.

What Jesus did on the cross means that we no longer have to focus on ourselves to find peace and fulfillment in life. "Die" in this hymn speaks to our dying to self, of letting go of the need to have our own way, which releases us from having to strive and from distress when things don't go our way. "Truly live" speaks to not being taken down when life's challenges come—and more, the fullness of life in Christ. We can transcend the challenges and troubles of life and have contentment and joy even when life takes difficult and unexpected turns.

In a culture that is becoming increasingly focused on "self" and doing what we want, this message is desperately needed. I know I feel the pull to "look out for number one" at the expense of all else. My clients also regularly struggle to find a way to get all of their needs met in a world that doesn't care about them.

So often we want others—our spouses, friends, families—to make us happy and meet our needs, and are exasperated when they simply can't. We may expect our jobs to fulfill us and take care of us. In reality, most companies care very little for individual employees. The bottom line and their ever-increasing expansion is their driving force, not the well-being of employees. So, we press harder to get what we want and what we believe we deserve. Unfortunately, this often leads to burn-out, anxiety, stress, broken relationships, and depression—the opposite of what we wanted to have.

What's worse, even some of our churches have forgotten the way to a meaningful life in Christ. During church services, we are bombarded with teaching on how we can have the life we want through rituals and religion or through having more faith and confidently claiming the life we think God wants us to have. We are told we need to do more and perform better or to pray more fervently for God to bless us. These approaches assume God has bought into the American dream (which on some levels is the Western dream) of the pursuit of happiness as the ultimate good.

This, too, results in disillusionment and discouragement when life doesn't work out the way we expect. In response, some Christians settle into mediocrity, never expecting more from God or their faith, while others walk away from God altogether. It doesn't have to be that way! God has a better way that delivers on its promise.

My message is not new; it comes from the pages of the New Testament itself. For centuries believers have grasped this concept of dying to self and having the fullness of life that we long for and so often miss today. "New" is not always better or more advanced. I, too, have wrestled with dying to self and now seek to live it to the full. This truth is so different from how we are constantly urged to live that we no longer receive it easily. Even after years of knowing the benefits of dying to self, I still find I need to wrestle it down again. I expect I will until I die, but it does get easier with practice.

Though this idea *is* biblical, it is jarring. It goes against our strong cultural cry to *hold tightly* to our lives and make them everything *we* can make them. We think we deserve success, that hard work should always be rewarded, that others should consider us and always treat us fairly, that we should not have to suffer real pain or sickness, and that with enough effort, research, and perseverance we can have it all and fix it all! We believe things should and will always progress and get better. The result is inner conflict when we read in the New Testament of letting go of having things our way, holding life *lightly,* and following Jesus where *He* leads. The independent, me-focused, self-preservation perspective that many of us embrace simply isn't in the Bible. As it turns out, it is *not* the way to happiness, fulfillment, and hope.

Added to this, many churches do not teach us about the value of dying to self. Often pastors, so desperately seeking to be relevant, fear teaching the hard truths that deliver the hope we long for. This message doesn't immediately make us feel good. The way of the cross is slow, painful, and difficult. However, it is also freeing, rewarding, and lasting in ways that immediate gratification cannot provide.

So we rarely experience the freedom that Scripture promises, the freedom to not have to strive, to love without needing to be loved back, to feel our worth and value regardless of our life circumstances, and to know we are accepted and ultimately are okay no matter what.

For more than a decade I have worked with hundreds of clients who struggle with living in our culture and living by what Scripture teaches. They have bought into the perception that God's goodness means He wants their lives to work out according to our cultural values, standards, or goals. When things don't, they blame themselves or others and seek ways to "do" more and "be" better within their own strength. They want me to show them how to make things work the way they want and expect—to make God bless, heal, help, in whatever way *they* want.

When they find out God is interested in something different, some resist, some refuse, and others begrudgingly enter the wrestling and dying process. They know they'll find it painful and discouraging. However, as they come to know God more and what Scripture really says, they are able to release the illusion of control and embrace the deeper change God is seeking to do in them. They feel lighter, freer, and more hopeful. Life circumstances may not have changed significantly, but they themselves have. They are able to deal with life with a sense of purpose and joy.

I have tried to have both my way and God's way, but kept returning to my glaring inconsistency. When I looked deeper at the disconnect between Scripture and our culture, both for myself and my clients, I came to the following conclusion. Since Scripture is still true today, it must be possible to experience what it promises. And conversely, perhaps our culture has it wrong. Perhaps the New Testament's upside down and backward approach of dying to self so we can really live *is* the answer. Then I had more questions: What does that mean? How can a 21st century Christian live *in* this world and not be *of* this world? My clients have similar questions and wonder if and how they can experience God's promises within the struggles of their own lives. Whether these promises really make a difference for them?

This book seeks to provide answers from a fellow journeyer—answers that will enlighten you, empower you, encourage you, and give you sustaining hope. I must warn you that the journey is not smooth or easy. I can also assure you with absolute confidence, it will be worth the journey and so much more.

Along with the explanations, I have included some examples from my own life and fictionalized examples from others of how dying and living play out in real life. I have also used common examples from my clients' experiences. However, because I hold client confidentiality so highly, I have only used examples that occur so frequently that many clients and many readers are likely to relate and feel I could be talking about them. I have intentionally left out unique stories or struggles. To help you engage in the process, I have discussion questions at the end of each chapter. Freedom *is* available to you!

Who Am I to Guide this Exploration?

Who am I to guide this exploration? Good question. I, like you, am an ordinary traveler on the journey of life. However, I have been given this incredible privilege to point the way to others. In addition to being able to draw on my own life experiences, I have the benefit of an education in two post-graduate programs in professional counseling from Tyndale Seminary and Liberty University. Both schools offered longer programs that ensured we learned the important techniques and theories of tested and proven psychotherapy models. They also required us to wrestle with how psychology complements, contrasts, and integrates with Scripture.

In my practice, I particularly connect with issues of personhood, the nature of and motivation of behaviors, how our family of origin and life experiences affect how we see the world, and how thoughts, emotions, physical health, and spirituality all work together. I am repeatedly inspired by the amazing synergy between God's truth and how our increasing knowledge of the brain confirms and conforms to Scripture's teaching.

I would not claim to be a faith expert, but I do have a deep and intimate relationship with God. I also have insights into church culture because of my training in theology, biblical interpretation, spiritual direction, history, and congregational organization. The combination of my journey with God and my training has enabled me to interact with and understand Christians from many denominations and faith traditions. I love finding ways to make sense of Scripture for my clients and helping them see how ancient texts really do apply to and transform life today.

What's Ahead for You?

This past March I had the exhilarating experience of taking a "ladder tour" in the Colossal Caves in Arizona. This tour was one level up in difficulty from the basic tour, which stayed on the paved path. Each of us were given a hardhat with a light on the front so we could see our path in the otherwise dark areas of the cave. At one point, our guide led us into a small crevice and had us turn off our lights. I had never experienced complete darkness before, but in the depth of the rock, the darkness and the silence were all-encompassing. The experience was disorienting and gave us a new respect for the need to follow our guide and maintain working equipment.

She then took us on an adventure through narrow passages, around blind corners, and across narrow rock bridges where we were unable to see bottom. At times we needed to shore up our courage to keep going. We climbed narrow ladders, shimmied on our stomachs through tight spaces, and wound our way around spectacular formations. Some of the climbs had no ladders so we had to stretch and use our muscles to lift ourselves to the next level. At one point, someone needed help because she couldn't reach the next platform. We worked together, though it was scary and uncertain at times. Even so, the excitement and exhilaration of exploring such untampered grandeur in the depth of the earth was incredible!

Similar to caving, the journey to freedom includes times that are frightening. Often, people are not sure they want to continue. Risk is involved. And yet, for everyone who has taken the risk and relinquished control to Jesus, the results are the same—freedom, deep peace, joy, and a profound trust in God.

As with caving, we accept the direction of our guide—of Jesus as our ultimate guide. Life challenges will continue, but this journey allows for a perspective change that makes it all, somehow, okay.

If you are willing, I will take you on the journey through "the valley of the shadow of death," in this case, death to self. You will learn about the challenges of our shared mistaken beliefs. We will traverse along the bottom through the dying to self and finally, climb up the other side to the new life.

Will you join me?

Part I

They Want Us to Believe What?

Let's begin this journey by orienting ourselves to our destination. This is not a book about how to fix your life circumstances and make everything okay in keeping with prevailing cultural norms. Instead, it is a guide on how to live fully and richly in God and deal with life's challenges by aligning ourselves with God's values and directions as He presents them in Scripture. This book will guide us as we trek down and through the valley of dying to self and up the other side to a renewed perception of God, ourselves, and the world. Because of that change, we will see life from God's vantage point and be empowered to overcome the trials of life with a renewed sense of hope, faith, strength, and joy, even if the content of our lives does *not* change.

This dying to self is about letting go of our preconceived ideas, beliefs, and rigidly held expectations of how life should turn out for us and adopting God's perspective. I use the term "dying" intentionally because it is painful and heart-wrenching. We naturally resist it. It is about letting Jesus be Lord of our lives.

Jesus spoke of dying to ourselves as a necessary part of life. In John 12:24–25, He predicted His own death and taught that we must let go of our grip on our own life if we are to follow Him. He said, "Truly, truly, I tell you, unless a kernel of wheat falls to the ground and dies, it remains only a seed; but if it dies, it bears much fruit. Whoever loves his life will lose it, but whoever hates his life in this world will keep it for eternal life." While this certainly speaks of physical death and the new life we will have with

Jesus in heaven, it also speaks of us not loving our earthly life so much that we put it before God.

In the process, we gain a freedom and a joy that life's trials cannot overpower. This is the "abundance" or "life to the full" that Jesus said He came to provide in John 10:10. We don't have to wait until heaven to attain it. However, the only way to have it now is through dying to self. Even so, it *is* worth it in the living!

Sadly, this teaching has been lost in most churches today. I believe that is due to the ever-pressing drive to have, do, and live more in our own strength, a mindset Western culture has embraced. Even as Christians, we have come to believe that we can and should do it all without depending on God. Sure, we worship Him and read His Word, but we believe that *actually* depending on Him (or anyone for that matter) is weak.

Many Christians don't want to let God take control of their lives and lead them places they may or may not feel comfortable; often more Christians outright reject the idea. Unfortunately, by refusing God's prescribed way, we forfeit the blessings that *He* wants to abundantly pour out on us. They may not always be the blessings *we* want Him to give us, but once we receive them, we realize they are far better than the ones we thought we wanted or deserved.

1

Impact of the World

A reasonable starting point for our journey is the seeming safety of our known experience—our cultural norms, our worldviews. I say "seeming safety" because our assumptions can be a stumbling block and put us out of alignment in our understanding of the calling and promises of Scripture. They can also leave us without adequate resources and support in a world where people see the world and experience life from different presuppositions. So often we feel lost because there are no longer any clear and agreed upon pathways to follow.

As Christians, we are not exempt from the significant cultural transitions that are affecting every level of religious, political, and societal life.[1] Depending on our generation—Baby Boomers and Generations X, Y, and Z—we have different assumptions. Added to that, we've been influenced by the overarching worldview shift from modernism to post-modernism in which personal experience and preference trump absolute truth and objective knowledge. All this can undermine our view of our faith, creating doubt because we so often take our worldviews for granted, never considering or evaluating them.

Our worldviews are the filters through which we interpret life, regardless of our awareness of them. When we passively allow our changing culture to freely inform our filters, then we are subject to seeing the world the way "they" want us to. As Christians, we need to be aware of the detours our culture would like to lead us down. We need to be intentional about letting Scripture and God's worldview inform our worldviews more persuasively.

This chapter will help you understand some of the belief systems that have affected our outlook on life, a view that we take for granted. It will enable you to take a longer look so you can read the terrain correctly. We begin by looking at the impact of the different generations. Each one has a subculture that influences how those in that generation interpret life and other people and it governs what they find important to seek out.

Baby Boomer Legacy

Over the last 50 years the Baby Boomer generation has affected so much of how we do life and experience the world. With their drive, focus and sheer numbers, they have created many firsts. If you're a Baby Boomer, born between 1946 to 1964, how has your worldview been shaped?

The Baby Boomers gained their name from the fact that there was an explosion in births after WWII. Many came of age during the period of political unrest between President John F. Kennedy's assassination and the Watergate scandal, where President Nixon attempted to cover up espionage activities related to his re-election and was subsequently pardoned by his successor, though it was clear that he had been involved at minimum in a cover-up campaign. As a result, Boomers tend to distrust institutions of society and are highly independent.

They entered the workforce during a time ready for development, growth, and increasing opportunities, and became highly motivated with an extremely strong work ethic. They want results and are willing to work long hours to get them.

Boomers want a better life and instead of looking to institutions or organized religion for change, they are committed to creating meaning and purpose through their own understanding and perseverance. As a group, they have brought innovation, advancement, and progress to business and technology.

Spiritually, their distrust of organized religion has affected the way the public at large understands God and the purpose of life. Their independence and self-determinism has been widely embraced in the spiritual and religious areas of life. At the same time, they seek to find deeper significance and ultimate meaning in life.[2] As a result of this fusion, over the last fifty years, our culture has experienced the emergence of religious syncretism and the creation of one's own spirituality where we can pick and choose what works best for us.

> Our worldviews are the filters through which we interpret life, regardless of our awareness of them.

Through the Internet, people can share more ideas and can incorporate them into their personal worldview without needing to conform to any one system of thought. This mesh of shared morality makes it difficult to hold a Christian perspective, particularly when so many people misunderstand Christianity as being intolerant and hateful.

If you are a Boomer, you were likely left to create your own meaning and purpose in life. Adopting a Christian worldview may have been challenging because many of your peers may have looked down on accepting biblical principles as truth. At the same time, your independence and determinism work for your benefit as you recognize your freedom to choose your own path, even when that path is one of traditional thought.

James is a 66-year-old Boomer who has committed his life to his career and making a difference in this world. He climbed the corporate ladder in finance and administration and sought to help his company and its employees succeed and be productive. As a Christian, he always tries to make good moral choices and his integrity has paid off. He is now a vice president in an industry leading company.

As James considers his future, he knows he is not ready for retirement, if it means doing nothing meaningful. Though he has his faith in the background, he has been more influenced by his generation's call for advancement, development, and independence; these things seemed to be more tangible ways to create meaning in his life. In business he has control and knows how to succeed. Life without that kind of meaning and control is disconcerting.

Added to that, while he loves his wife dearly, his work has been his focus for so long that they are not as close as he had thought they would be at this stage. If he were honest with himself, the idea of being home all day together and having nothing to do scares him.

Generation X Contribution

Members of Generation X were born roughly between 1961 and 1981[3] and as a group are relatively small in number. Gen Xers grew up as the first "latch-key" generation with many having both parents working outside of the home. This meant they had a lot of freedom growing up and were generally left to fend for themselves.

When they came of age, the economic world was in a financial downturn, jobs were hard to find, and they could not expect jobs for life. These were challenging times and, once again, they were left to fend for themselves.

In this environment, their skepticism and even stronger individualism grew. They believe it is up to them to make things happen and don't expect to have life made easy. This skepticism and individualism make it extremely challenging for them to consider depending on God in any real way. With many of their parents working so much and living life on their own terms, many Gen Xers have never witnessed what depending on God in everyday life looks like.

At the same time, they are at home with technological advancement, being the first generation to grow up with microwaves and remote control television. As a result, they expect things immediately, and want instant gratification.

An overarching attitude of this generation is skepticism of others in general. Gen Xers are less willing to simply follow without having a clear understanding of where they are being led and why it is advantageous. They want to know what the outcome will be before they put in the effort. There must be some value for them in the end. They embrace access to information through the Internet and will research on their own before accepting what others tell them.

They embrace excitement and challenge, like extreme sports, and are not afraid to push themselves or to create their own reality. Christianity can be difficult for members of this generation because they feel it restricts them instead of providing the instant satisfaction they long for. They need to see how following Jesus affects real life and makes things better in the now. These Christians are not satisfied with or interested in the heaven-focused perspective that many churches preach so often. Their faith can become sidelined. However, they are quite open and eager to experience God in personal ways and when they do they are passionate about finding ways to make it relevant in their daily lives.

Chris is forty-six. He graduated from university with an English degree and continued to work at the university bookstore because he his education wasn't opening any other doors for him. After three years of that, he had had enough and moved back home with his mom so he could go back to school for something that could get him a job.

His degree in computer sciences meant he could get an entry-level position at a large company. Hoping for advancement and not wanting to burden his mom, he moved out and tried to pay down his student loan. Like many in his generation, with the Boomers holding higher positions and the economy in a downturn, he found little room for advancement, so paying off his debt had stalled. After five years, he decided to open his own business.

Around that time he met and married Sandra, who also had school and consumer debt. Even so, they decided to invest in the business.

After eight years he was doing fairly well, and with Sandra's teaching salary they finally purchased their first home. Now, five years later with two growing children, they are feeling the financial pressure of saving for their children's education and their own retirement.

Now Chris is looking for something more but is at a loss as to where to look. An old friend had taken him to church years ago but somehow it didn't seem relevant to real life. He doesn't want religion that will restrict him and not add value to his life. Even so, he recognizes he is looking for something spiritual that would make a difference in his life. He doesn't expect anything to be simply given to him; life has taught him that things don't work that way. He's skeptical that there really is anything to it but thinks there is no harm in looking. So, he begins his spiritual search by investigating what's out there on the Internet.

The Millennials Advance

Generation Y, or the Millennials, are said to have been born between 1981 and 2001 and the Millennial generation is almost as large as the Boomer generation. Less is known about Generation Z as they are only now coming of age. The Millennial generation has continued the move away from institutional values. But, instead of focusing on independence, they are more communal and collaborative.[4] Most of them have only known life with cable TV, computers, and cell phones. They are extremely tech-savvy.

At the same time, Millennials grew up with helicopter parents who over affirmed them, constantly involved them in organized activities, and stayed connected with them at all times. This has left Millennials needing more constant affirmation and feedback from authority figures, and yet less equipped to receive constructive feedback or criticism.

Millennials are also confident in their own ideas and self-worth and do not shy away from expressing their opinions. They expect to be listened to and valued, even before they have done anything to prove themselves.

Millennials, being used to constant change, embrace a flexible lifestyle. While they fully expect great things from life, they are not willing to sacrifice self-fulfillment to achieve success.

For them, the great things of life include family, friends, and a balance between work and entertainment. In fact, they would prefer to work smarter, not harder, and expect that to be possible in all cases. They have been told, and many fully believe, they can have it all—or at least that they should be able to.

Because they grew up in an Internet environment, they are adept at sifting through vast volumes of information quickly and efficiently. As a result, they are also marked by reduced commitment and lack of ability to persevere. Many devour information but are not equipped to apply it.

Their relationships are characterized by quantity more than depth or quality. Millennials are often more comfortable interacting remotely rather than face-to-face and can struggle to have meaningful conversations or know people intimately.

This difficulty in being able to build meaningful interpersonal connections affects their well-being and emotional stability. One writer noted that in 2009 the general population of students was "less mentally healthy" than those in 1969.[5] Finding truth, security, purpose, and real community where they can be known is becoming harder and harder.

Amanda is a 24-year-old Millennial living with her parents and doing her best to figure out how to be an adult and make a life for herself. She went to university to be a teacher, but no one was hiring teachers when she graduated.

She is currently a server at a trendy restaurant, and as with many of her generation, moving into her own home will not be possible anytime soon. She has considered going back to school or looking for something else other than teaching. At the same time, she lacks the motivation needed to put in that kind of effort, and her parents can't afford to help her financially with another degree.

Amanda knows she needs to move forward to establish her own life, but still enjoys the freedoms of living at home where mom and dad pay the bills. Having to put up with her parents' hovering is annoying but manageable at this point—at least until she can really get life going.

Though she was brought up in a Christian home, when she went to university and was out from under her parents' constant watch, she strayed from her faith and made new friends who did not share her Christian beliefs; now she is trying to get back to Jesus and her faith. The challenge is that she still really likes her old ways, and her friends at school did not see them as wrong. In fact, they thought she was "conservative" compared to the things they were doing, and now they don't understand her return to God at all. Even so, at this point Amanda's Christianity is more related to reconnecting with her church friends than making her faith her own.

At the same time, she often struggles with conflict in her friendship circles. She wants closer connections but isn't quite sure how to have them. When she is not at work or with her friends, she stays in touch with them through social media, regularly posting so they can always know what's going on. Though staying connected and informed are extremely important to her, she is beginning to notice there is always drama of some kind going on with her friends.

Amanda's Christian friends don't know about her university lifestyle and are focused on finding husbands. Some have found one and are struggling in their marriages. Even so, she feels the pressure to find her soul mate. She is on a Christian dating site and is looking for a good Christian man to marry. But she is not sure how to do that in Christian circles where casual dating is less common. This isn't how she thought her life would be.

Discussion Questions

1. Identify the characteristics of your generation that resonate with your own perceptions and ways of interacting in your world.

2. Consider the other generations described, and reflect on the differences you have noticed in interacting with people in these cohorts.

3. In light of what you have just read, consider how the values of your generation may have affected your perceptions of God and the church.

2

Shifting Roadmaps

In addition to being shaped by the generations we were born into, we are deeply influenced by the meta-cultural shift of the last century. The change in the prevailing Western philosophy from modernism to post-modernism has affected basic values and how many of us experience life. A brief exploration of this shift will help you better understand why some of your experiences and your understanding of the promises of Scripture rarely align. This will then allow you to evaluate your presuppositions and consider new ways of seeing the world that will enable you to align with God's worldview more effectively and confidently.

Modernism

A modern worldview is based on Judeo-Christian values. This includes the idea that absolute truth exists and is knowable, that there is one God, and that the Bible is a reliable reference point for life. In this worldview, logic and rational thought are the framework for learning, and it assumes that the world can be broken down systemically and is understandable. Institutions are regarded as a good and trustworthy way of organizing and serving people. Those shaped by a modern worldview live life in the local arena and allow community systems to govern day-to-day life.

Many Baby Boomers have this overarching mindset. But a significant number, about one third, have a more post-modern than modern view.[6] Some Gen Xers also hold this view even though that generation has been heavily influenced by this paradigm shift. Thus, generation alone is not a reliable guide as to where a person may fall within these two viewpoints.

My husband, a Gen Xer, maintains a strong modern worldview. He is very logic based and sees very little value in finding truth through experiential knowledge. The Bible is the moral compass he follows and he views any truth related to healthy living that is not clearly supported in Scripture as unnecessary, at best. Supernatural experiences are questionable and must be strictly evaluated through traditional systematic theology. For him as a modern, they certainly are not required or to be relied upon within the Christian faith.

Post-modernism

In a post-modern mindset absolute truth no longer exists. There are no agreed upon overarching principles that everyone is expected to adhere to. Only high-level absolutes that serve the community remain, such as murder and extreme violence being wrong. Beyond that, post-moderns derive their morals and ethics from the media and their peers.

Thus, the Bible is regarded as a religious book but one with no more authority than any other book. Monotheism has given way to an acceptance of many gods and many ways of accessing the spiritual. Further, post-moderns value experience and mysticism more than fact-based religious systems. Even within Christianity, there is an increased interest in religious experience and less in doctrine and apologetics. Christianity is generally looked upon as a judgmental, intolerant, and hypocritical religion.

Appreciation for diversity within a global context and for differing perspectives is highly valued. In this environment, people determine what works for them and their understanding is more important than systematized or organized beliefs. Logic and rational thought are considered a less reliable way of gaining knowledge than personal experience.

This can undermine Christians' confidence in Scripture and what we are taught. Or worse, we can end up being taught by pastors who don't hold to Christian values. Staying true to God's Word in a post-modern culture is challenging because we are being told by our society that the Bible is no more valid than any other religious book and even that we are just plain wrong.

Many Christians who are strongly post-modern can tend to chase after spiritual experiences where they can really "feel" God's presence and leading. When that feeling is not there, they either question their relationship with Him or head out in search of another church or conference where they can feel Him again.

Where do Christians go now?

In today's world, where can Christians find hope? I truly do not believe Christianity is ill equipped for this life. Christianity was birthed in a time of similar transition. Jesus brought about this transition as He fulfilled the prophecies of the Old Testament. Many people were not ready to accept the shift and resisted Him and His followers, and yet Jesus encouraged His followers to stand firm in the truth, even as the world rejected them. Jesus' urging to stand firm also applies to us as our culture moves ever further from Christianity.

In our own lives and in our churches, many of us have become lax about the foundational teachings of Jesus and the Bible. As our faith has merged with our culture, we have lost some of the power and hope that Jesus' message brings. Our focus has become our happiness and our prosperity, even in matters of faith, rather than our surrender to Jesus who knows what is best for us. However, we can return to our roots in how we engage in our faith and still be able to live in our world rather than totally separate from it.

> Our focus has become our happiness and our prosperity, even in matters of faith, rather than our surrender to Jesus.

This has been the case for me. I'm a Gen Xer and tend to be more post-modern than modern in my worldview. However, as a devoted Christ-follower, my perspective is tempered. I find there *is* absolute truth found in God. Unfortunately, we don't have as much access to it as the moderns would suggest. There is not enough time, effort, or logic available in this world to make His mysteries knowable. As post-moderns suggest, we can learn from experience and in matter-of-fact ways.

I maintain that many things are unknowable and impact much of how we experience life. As soon as an experience occurs, the facts of it are skewed by our perception. In my work and relationships, I see relativity at play and how perspective changes the way we experience life. This is why I find it is so important to continually seek out truth and gain as much of God's perspective as possible.

I feel comfortable with highly valuing experiential knowledge, because I see it as an integral part of our faith journey with God. He speaks through the Bible *and* through our experiences. I also defer to biblical truth as the source and evaluator of experience. If something goes against Scripture, then Scripture has the authority over experience, even when it goes against my cultural sensitivities. You will see more of how this works as we continue our journey.

Discussion Questions

1. Do you resonate more with seeing the world as a Modern or a Post-Modern? Why? Remember, your generation does not necessarily determine this.

2. Consider how your way of seeing the world may have affected your perceptions of God and the church.

3. When have you navigated a situation where your faith and your worldview have been in conflict? How have you handled that?

4. Take time to pray and ask God to show you any areas in your life where your worldview has negatively influenced your faith or moved you away from biblical truth. Journal about this and invite God to help you bring your perspective (and behavior, if applicable) more in line with His.

3

In the Church

Before we move on in our journey, let's do a little more preparation and explore our church culture and what many of us experience there. Before we can readily learn what makes our Christian faith sustainable in a post-modern world, we must first understand some of the beliefs found in our churches and how our churches' culture affects us.

Our churches play a key role in shaping what we seek in life and how we try to get it, particularly in relation to God. Stepping back to explore what many teach will enable us to make informed decisions about how we want to move forward with God and our churches. We don't have to blindly follow, assuming we are going where God wants us to go.

To begin this exploration, let's consider the two extremes of what people seek church and God for. For many people, church and God are mainly about figuring out how to get into heaven or avoid hell, once they die. For others, the focus may be on social justice and trying to create a moral society. Both perspectives have strengths and both miss the crux of the Gospel and what it really offers us.

In *The Divine Conspiracy*, Dallas Willard provides insights into the two main Western perspectives on Christianity: theologically liberal left and conservative right. Whether we are in a liberal or conservative church, our beliefs are centered on how to deal with the problem of sin. In *My Utmost for His Highest*, Oswald

Chambers defines sin as "a fundamental relationship; it is not wrong doing, it is wrong *being*, deliberate and emphatic independence of God." He contrasts sins of behavior with sin as a state of being.

Thus, sin can be defined biblically as anything that goes against what God says we should *do* or *be*. Scripture tells us that "all have sinned and fall short of the glory of God" (Romans 3:23) and that "the wages of sin is death, but the gift of God is eternal life in Christ Jesus our Lord" (Romans 6:23). We understand this to mean that because of our inherited sin nature and the sinful behaviors prompted by our nature (falling short of the glory of God), we deserve death and hell (the alternative to eternal life with Jesus).

Thus, what we do about the problem of sin is a key part of what churches must address. In fact, our beliefs about sin will determine how we live as Christians. Many churches focus on sin as behavior rather than on the ultimate focus of sin as an inherited state of being that we cannot change as humans.

Those in liberal churches put the emphasis on living a good and socially ethical life in the now. Scripture does provide strong support for living a socially ethical life. James 1:27 says, "Religion that God our Father accepts as pure and faultless is this: to look after orphans and widows in their distress and to keep oneself from being polluted by the world." Further, Jesus taught about the division of the sheep and goats (referring to those saved and those who will spend eternity in hell, respectively) and said,

> Come, you who are blessed by my Father; take your inheritance, the kingdom prepared for you since the creation of the world. For I was hungry and you gave me something to eat, I was thirsty and you gave me something to drink, I was a stranger and you invited me in, I needed clothes and you clothed me, I was sick and you looked after me, I was in prison and you came to visit me... whatever you did for one of the least of these brothers and sisters of mine, you did for me. (Matthew 25:34–39)

Thus, for the liberal Christian, the focus is on human rights and fighting for justice, and not necessarily on salvation. In this view, biblical requirements for accepting Jesus as the only way have been minimized and, in some cases, set aside. Rather, true Christianity cares for the down-trodden, the under privileged, and the oppressed. In the liberal view, Jesus is held up as the ultimate example of love, and Christians are to emulate Him by acts of love to show the world that God *is* Love. Further, the thought is that if people would stop judging others and learn to accept and embrace one another, God's love would rule on earth and sin would be dealt with lovingly. People would get along better and sin against others would decrease or be eliminated.

However, as Willard suggests, "We have from the Christian left, after all, just another gospel of sin management, but one whose substance is provided by Western (American) social and political ideals of human existence in a secular world." The problem is that this perspective focuses on more secondary issues from Jesus' teaching, while missing His central and foundational teachings—He came to bring salvation to the world and to create disciples (Christians who are devoted to Him and follow Him by being in a dependent relationship with Him).

By contrast, those in conservative congregations put the emphasis on salvation, receiving forgiveness and having "saving" faith, because our sin separates us from God and excludes us from heaven. For the conservative Christian, Jesus died so that we could be forgiven, receive salvation (entrance into heaven), and become like Him. For some churches, salvation is the key focus, for others, "saving" faith is faith that proves itself through actions. Thus, within the conservative perspective, there are variations and different aspects of salvation and saving faith that are emphasized.

In the churches where entrance into heaven is the primary goal, the crux of salvation is receiving forgiveness for sin and gaining entrance into heaven based on God's grace. Here they would argue for "grace alone," meaning that people only need to recognize their sin as being wrong, separating them from God, and accept Jesus' sacrifice to deal with and pay the penalty for their sin. "Christian living" is seen as important and so there will be teaching on following Jesus' example and the principles of right living in the Bible, but more important is their eternal destination.

In this perspective, once someone has become a Christian, they are expected to attend church and join activities that are part of church living. This is evidence that they are Christians and the expectation is that they will want to do this simply because they made this decision to accept forgiveness. Such participation is not stressed as a requirement. As a result, while many Christians in this camp are thankful to know their eternal destination is secure, they do not necessarily focus on living their faith outside of church. They view church life as separate from work, friends, family, or other activities.

Because the teaching they receive does not stress the importance of dependence on Jesus in all aspects of life, they do not realize they are missing something significant. While they have invited Jesus into their spiritual lives, they are limiting His impact in other areas.

I like to use the example of our lives as a house. When we accept Jesus as our savior, He moves into the house and takes legal ownership. However, He is always a gentleman and does not go beyond the front hall unless we invite Him to go further. He will not force His legal right to bring order to the house in any rooms that we do not let Him in to. Most Christians are content to leave Jesus in the front hall.

Consequently, when life challenges them, they may not realize that God's complete involvement is a resource. They forget He owns the house and is fully capable of organizing it in the best way for them. Often Christians will blame God and struggle with understanding how He would allow a problem when they have done all that is *required* but not allowed Him to take full occupancy. They expect that He will simply protect the outside of the house while they control the inside.

For those who emphasize saving faith as evidence for salvation, the idea of Lordship (or God becoming Lord and Master of one's life) is a necessary next step after receiving forgiveness of sins. Living one's Christianity in the now is of paramount importance. While their overarching focus is on receiving forgiveness and entrance to heaven, the Lordship requirement means living life in a way that will *ensure* entrance to heaven. This involves obeying Jesus' teachings. Adherents to this perspective teach that saving faith *proves* itself through someone obeying biblical principles and commands.

These churches believe that the salvation of those who do not live in accordance with the Bible and the teachings of the church remains in question. Much of what is said in the Lordship perspective makes sense and, in fact, is quite biblical. In James chapter 2, James speaks forcefully of the relationship between faith and works and proclaims that faith without works is dead.

At the same time, these churches affirm that works do not provide entrance to heaven; it is a free gift. In this perspective, it is understood that Christians *should* look and behave differently in response to the forgiveness they have received. This is supported in Scripture through passages like Matthew 7:18–20, ESV:

> A healthy tree cannot bear bad fruit, nor can a diseased tree bear good fruit. Every tree that does not bear good fruit is cut down and thrown into the fire. Thus you will recognize them by their fruits.

The focus and effort of people with this perspective can inadvertently become directed to proving that their faith is real through looking the way they are expected to look.

Unfortunately, most who become Christians within these churches are not clearly told about these expectations beforehand. They are told that grace cannot be earned and is a free gift from God. Then, when they become Christians, they are informed of this new "requirement" to look the part. When many of these Christians struggle to overcome their sin or are not living up to the expectations of their church or what they understand God wants of them, they end up questioning whether their salvation is real.

What do we say initially?

Once again, while the teachings within the conservative church are biblical, they too often miss the key focus of Jesus' teaching. This is that God is less interested in people's external behavior and is much more interested in the changes that occur on the inside. Such changes will, in turn, become evident in external behavior without the person having to make extreme efforts.

At age sixteen, I became a Christian to gain salvation because I did not want to go to hell. It wasn't until I was in my mid-twenties that my view of God shifted from Him being merely savior to being Lord. At that point, I knew I needed to align my behaviors with my professed beliefs, and I had to start following what the Bible said. I knew what I had been doing wasn't enough, so I sought to understand what else God was asking of me.

The shortcoming with the focus on behavior is that it does not take into consideration the starting point of the Christian's heart when they were saved or the motivation and activating power behind their external changes.

> God is less interested in people's external behavior and is much more interested in the changes that occur on the inside.

In *Mere Christianity*, C.S. Lewis brings this home when he talks about a particularly well dispositioned man compared with an inherently nasty woman. Their natural personality tendencies do not prove or disprove salvation or what God is or is not doing in their lives. Both need to surrender their wills and natures to God and allow Him to change them. On the surface, the evidence may look more significant in the woman than the man, but God is most interested in them surrendering and allowing Him to bring about change.

For many years, Linda, a sixty-year-old nurse, attended the conservative Christian church she grew up in. During those years she learned what Christians should look like and always strived to please God. But, after five years of marriage to a man who constantly tore her down, she felt that God didn't seem to be there for her or care if she was losing herself.

She looked for help from her church but the leaders didn't understand and insisted she must stay and submit to her husband, an outwardly upstanding Christian and devoted member of the church. Within the church, he did everything well and seemed to be a mature Christian. The leaders would not believe that he could be so different at home. Finally, she threw her husband out. The church shunned her. It didn't matter that he treated her horribly; divorce was a sin.

She was again counseled to put up with his repeatedly demeaning treatment of her by "turning the other cheek" and praying for him. They suggested she was exaggerating the situations and needed to look at her own attitudes and behavior. They said evidence of a truly repentant heart would be her following their directives and what they insisted the Bible required of her.

When she would not do that, she was brought before the church for discipline, and her membership was taken from her. As she left the church that day, she vowed to never return. Now Linda sees herself as "evolved" and is always accepting of others—everyone except Christians, who represent how badly she was treated when she needed them most.

Discussion Questions

1. How would you describe your church in terms of being on the liberal left versus the conservative right? Or are they somewhere in the middle? How has that influenced you?

2. How does your church address sin? Do you find them supportive, directive, or dismissive in their approach?

3. Where does your church fall in the Lordship debate? Do they make a distinction between gaining access into heaven and living as though Jesus is Lord of your behaviors? How has that influenced you?

4

Beyond Lordship
to Discipleship

To further map out our journey toward freedom, we need to explore the Lordship perspective in comparison to Jesus' invitation to discipleship.

While the Lordship perspective has validity, it can take Christians off course ever so slightly, but still enough for Christians to miss God's intended destination. Specifically, two subtle, but powerful problems can put us off course: 1) institutionalizing the need for works to prove our faith and 2) focusing on the works that we can do *for* God rather than on allowing Him to prompt and empower the works we do. These result in Christians that lack the knowledge or resources they need to rely on the power of the Holy Spirit who is our ever-present resource.

As the ideal of the Lordship perspective became institutionalized, churches began to add to what God taught about salvation. The focus shifted away from God to the importance of keeping the laws and the traditions set out by the religious leaders and institutions. Religion overshadowed God.

Bruxy Cavey defines "religion" as "any *reliance* on systems or institutions, rules or rituals as our *conduit to* God" (emphasis mine).[7] Within the Church, many denominations would say that Jesus is the way to God, but then they overlay theology and put the emphasis on viewpoints that often end up communicating that the way to God is Jesus along with other requirements; those can include baptism, church attendance, membership, behaviors, attitudes, changes, giving, and/or spiritual gifting.

As a result, when someone asks Jesus for forgiveness and receives salvation, they are expected to fulfill additional requirements. If they don't, their *true* salvation is brought into question. This leads to confusion, guilt, and doubt for many new believers. Others simply conform and learn to "walk-the-walk" and "talk-the-talk", not really knowing whether they are doing enough or have changed enough to evidence *real* saving grace.

These Christians don't experience the liberation Jesus intends for them. Instead of freedom and empowerment, they are shackled with expectations and requirements to prove themselves without ever being taught how they are to achieve what God is asking of His people. They see God as a task master who will judge and reject them when they fall back into old sins or struggle to fulfill the requirements of the church or even the Bible.

They may also be led to expect that if they are able to conform to many of the requirements, life will turn out well for them. God is expected to bless them. The argument goes, if I do all that is expected of me, then God should hold up His end of the bargain and protect me from undue hardship, trials, and suffering.

Even Christians who have genuinely accepted Christ as their personal savior and live comfortably within the religious confines they respect are not prepared when life stops being what they perceive as good. Any setback goes against the pervasive belief system that says right living means being spared from serious trials and pain. They've been taught that life will go well and God will "work things out" for the faithful.

While they know that they could face persecution and ordeals related to being followers of Jesus because that's what the Bible says, it's a remote possibility. At this point in history, in North America, Christians are rarely persecuted and most of us live relatively comfortable lives. As Christians living in a rich environment that promotes forward motion, prosperity, and the pursuit of happiness, we can be affected by the assumptions of our culture. We believe God wants prosperity and happiness for Christians even more than for the general public because we belong to Him. We want this for our children, so we think that God must want this for us. So, it's been easy for the belief to take hold that Christians should be safe and God should make things run smoothly for us when we ask Him to—unless we have significantly disappointed Him, of course.

Unfortunately, when faced with hardships, many Christians automatically ask questions because of this mistaken belief like: What did I do to deserve this? What sin is God punishing me for? Perhaps I don't have enough faith or real saving faith. We may call God's goodness and grace into question. It is human nature to try to make sense of pain and suffering but the expectation that God will protect us *as we want Him to* takes us off course.

This teaching has left these Christians without a framework to make sense of the suffering that inevitably comes their way. If they had been taught that at the fall of humanity, suffering became part of everyone's normal experience, and that Jesus' coming does not change that until His second coming, they would not be so shocked and disoriented when they encounter difficulties.

Further, these believers do not have support within their church because of current church culture regarding pain. Many Christian churches expect that real Christians should be able to handle anything without struggle and that if they have a problem, God will give them joy and peace that surpasses understanding and so they won't feel pain.

As a result, many Christians do not reveal to others that they are deeply suffering for fear of judgment. Or, they don't allow themselves to admit they are suffering for fear that their faith is not real. They end up suffering even more, and are cut off from the community that God intended to help them bear their suffering.

Unfortunately, people only take to heart passages in the Bible that seem to support this thinking and ignore those that provide a more realistic picture of life that includes trials and suffering. Yes, Philippians 4:7 does say, "And the peace of God, which surpasses all understanding, will guard your hearts and your minds in Christ Jesus." Some interpret this as meaning that God will protect them from feeling deep distress.

Because of the *mistaken* belief that becoming a Christ-follower means your life should always work out well, Christians can view God as less relevant, inaccessible, and untrustworthy in the face of difficulties that shake them. They don't understand that the verse means that the peace that surpasses understanding is a calm that *accompanies* deep pain and suffering as we authentically walk through it.

> The peace that surpasses understanding is a calm that *accompanies* deep pain and suffering as we authentically walk through it.

Jennifer (Jen), a thirty-eight-year-old business woman, grew up in a strong Christian home. She became a Christian at twelve, and has never wavered from her faith. Life has not been easy though. Her older brother, who was the shining star in the family, succeeded in every area and she was left to struggle in his shadow.

Always longing for acceptance and approval from her workaholic and perfectionistic parents, she pushed through school and started her own consulting business right out of university. When her frequent traveling kept her from settling down and having a family, she took a position at a local company, but it didn't work out. After she earned an MBA, she landed a promising job as a human resources manager but after a few years the company was bought out and employees let go.

Throughout it all, she continued to attend her family church when she was in town, and she served on different committees and ministries within her church body. In her work she remained ethical and openly shared her faith when people were open to hear it. Even while she was in school she committed to God to take a Sabbath on Sundays so she could continue to serve God and be involved in the church.

At this point, she feels like she has been doing everything she can to please her parents, her church, and her God.

Each Sunday, Jen goes to church and sees people's lives running smoothly. Things are falling into place the way they should be for them. Clearly she must be doing *something* wrong, but she is doing all that she knows how to do. It just isn't working.

Friends are praying for her, but no one can understand why she isn't married, and why things don't ever seem to work out for her. After all, she is friendly, attractive, generous, and devoted to her church. Well-meaning people tell her it's only a matter of time, but in her eyes, time is running out. *None of this seems fair. Where is God in all of this? Does He even care about her? What more could she do to gain His approval so that her life can finally start working out the way it is supposed to?*

The second problem that arises out of Lordship, as it is often preached, is that it does not provide us any resources or hope for living well in the now. The emphasis on God providing for the future and us living in response to what He has done suggests that God is not involved in how we live now. While a church might say God is involved and helps us, many don't make it clear how He does it. Perhaps we are told to pray and serve and yet the focus remains on us doing *for* Him. However, we are not capable of doing all that is laid out in Scripture without *God* working in us.

Most of our churches also function in their own power. Church leaders pray and seek God's leading and once they feel they have received it, they take control and do what they think is best to work out the plan or vision. Reliance quickly shifts to strategic plans and systems instead of actual dependence on God to work it out step by step. This is not to say plans are not valuable; it is to reveal a lack of recognition that all plans must be held lightly and remain open to God's redirection at any time.

Thus, if our churches and church leaders are acting in their own power, it is not surprising that most Christians believe this is how they are to live out their life as Christians. In essence, many Christians pray for His blessing rather than His leading.

At salvation, God gave us the ability to work in the power of the Holy Spirit but not to use that power at our discretion. The Holy Spirit is a person we are to be in relationship with and *submission to*. He does not empower us to take control from Him or to use His power while excluding Him.

God working *in* us is a spiritual concept that is at odds with our culture's emphasis on control being in *our* hands. Many churches have not taught this and we do not recognize that we must *tap into* the power of the Holy Spirit to be able to do what God requires of us. This empowerment comes from being in actual relationship with God and regularly seeking out His leading and plans within our day-to-day activities. As we rely on Him, He *empowers* us to do what He is asking of us. If He doesn't empower us, He may not be leading us where we think He is leading.

The focus must shift from what *we* think we need to be doing to allowing *Him* to lead and change us. Even those who've been taught about the empowering of the Holy Spirit and the resources he has for us, find giving control to Him very uncomfortable.

We have reached the valley floor now. Shall we explore further?

Discussion Questions

1. In your own faith journey, what role does Jesus play? Is He merely savior or does He have your permission to affect your life in the living? Have you considered what it would mean for Him to become Lord of your life? How would things change for you if He were Lord?

2. How do you go about living out your faith? Do you find you are trying to please God with your behavior and faithfulness? Do you pray and ask for His direction? What do you do when you feel you receive His direction?

Part II

What Foolishness is This?

Here, at the valley floor, you may feel disoriented and a little uncertain. Now that our carefully constructed ideals about our culture and how it influences us have been brought into question, we are left to face our reality. Before we move across the valley though, it's wise to check our expectations for life because they help set our direction. Or, as King Solomon would say, we will look at life "under the sun."

For most people this tends to be one of the hardest parts of the journey. The beginning of our death to self starts with letting go of our ideals and unrealistic expectations; it involves changing our view of God and our attitudes toward problems. Throughout this section we will learn more about ourselves as we compare many of our expectations with the teachings of King Solomon and the New Testament.

From there, we will dig into the character and ways of God to reveal something that is completely counter-cultural and yet surprisingly restorative. Know that we are never alone. We will do this together with Jesus. While reality is often difficult to face, remember, the truth *will* set us free.

5

Life Under the Sun

As we begin this next leg of our journey, it makes sense to begin with King Solomon's perspective on life in the now, or as he would call it in the book of Ecclesiastes, "life under the sun". In Ecclesiastes, one of the wisdom books in the Old Testament, the king provides readers with his insights on what's happening when things seem to make no sense. The Teacher (King Solomon) says from the start, "Meaningless! Meaningless! ... Utterly meaningless! Everything is meaningless" (1:2).

Throughout the book, the Teacher compares the lives of the righteous and the wicked and discovers very little difference between them. In fact, he notes in 8:14, "There is something else meaningless that occurs on earth: the righteous who get what the wicked deserve, and the wicked who get what the righteous deserve." Though this is not fair, and we could argue it *should not* be this way, King Solomon rightly observed, this *is* how life goes, at least some of the time.

He says that there is a time for everything in life, and no one has any control over when the times of trials or peace will come. In 7:14, he says, "Therefore, no one can discover anything about their future." We are not meant to know our futures or be able to control how things turn out. That is within God's control.

That is the rub. We want to make God into a tame being, who only brings what we deem to be good and fair. From this perspective He becomes the one to serve us, and not the other way around. May it never be! God is God, and He is not here to make things work out for *us*. That likely sounds harsh but it truly is not. God is good and He loves us more than we can ever comprehend, but we won't always understand how He works. Centuries later, Isaiah reminded us in verse 55:8, "'For my thoughts are not your thoughts, neither are your ways my ways,' declares the LORD."

While I have not faced the extreme trials that some people face, I have faced challenges. In my teens and early twenties, though I had accepted Jesus as my savior, I had not learned to live a life that was marked by my faith. I was independent and determined to live life my way. I did not want or need others telling me what I could and couldn't do and that included God to a certain extent. My faith was about getting into heaven and I continued to try to live a good Christian life the way I defined it. My Christianity did not assist, in any way, with the real life challenges I faced. I simply wanted God to make things better for me while I continued to live the life I wanted to live. This is not His way, as I found out.

Both high school and college years were challenging for me. My sister seemed to succeed in most things and always seemed more popular and put together than I was. Though I tried to do well, my marks were never as good. My parents would tell me not to compare myself to her, but I did. I wanted my sister's approval and validation more than anyone else's. However, when I tried to talk to her about my struggles, she never seemed to understand and would often say my life was not that difficult.

Though I always had friends, I never seemed to really fit in well even in college. From my perspective, I didn't fit anywhere. I know my own insecurities contributed to this perception but no matter what I did, I always seemed to be somewhere on the outside looking in.

I did not fit well in my college program either. Somewhere in the middle of my second year I noticed my marks were dropping and after trying a number of things, I went to a professor, who was also the dean, and let him know that I wanted to complete this program. I was willing to do whatever it took, including extra help and extra work. I feared failure because I didn't see any other valid option for my future if I didn't complete the program.

Surprisingly, my marks stabilized, but I never excelled, that is until an AutoCAD course really connected for me. Many others were struggling with it, which added to my feeling of being different. But, that course landed me my first career job in facilities management.

Unfortunately, I floundered in that job. My social life had dwindled to minimal friendships, a distant relationship with my sister, who lived on the other side of town, and with my parents who had moved a two-hour-flight away. I lived with a roommate who I only occasionally got along with. "My way" hadn't worked at all!

In Ecclesiastes, Solomon also deals with our expectations for satisfaction in life. We try sex, power, and money, but they leave us unsatisfied. Our attempts are

> We want to make God into a tame being, who only brings what we deem to be good and fair.

futile, points out the Teacher. He repeats the term "under the sun" to reinforce that the way we experience life is the way people before us have always experienced it. Verse 1:9 says, "What has been will be again, what has been done will be done again; there is nothing new under the sun." With our limited perspective, we can only gain or observe human wisdom. King Solomon, however, plumbed the depths of wisdom. When we are unable to see or understand what God sees and orchestrates beyond our temporal existence, we are left with a world that is unfair and meaningless. If there were nothing beyond this earth, all *would* be futile.

Solomon's solution to dealing with our problems is not to try to make sense of inconsistencies and unfairness, but to focus on God. The difficulties and letdowns of life rarely make sense, particularly when we are in the midst of them. Therefore, the Teacher suggests in verse 7:14 that we change our thinking about the situation. He declares, "When times are good, be happy; but when times are bad, consider this: God has made the one as well as the other."

Much research in modern psychology supports the idea that what we focus on affects our *experience* of what we deal with. From that has come the understanding that when we learn to think about things differently, our experience of the situation or interaction changes.

Imagine that you run into an old friend in a hotel lobby, who you have not seen for years. When you say hello and try to talk, they brush you off and run out of the hotel. Naturally, you feel slighted and a bit offended. However, once you find out that they were searching for their six-year-old child, your experience of the interaction changes. You are no longer offended and in fact, are willing to help them find their lost loved one.

We cannot change much of the content of our life. However, there are often many different ways of looking at things and possible explanations for why things turn out the way they do. Unfortunately for many of us, God is the only one who fully sees the whole picture and can make sense of what is going on and He rarely shares His perspective with us in the midst of it. Even so, our intentional effort to look at different aspects of a situation can affect how we feel about the situation.

Further, research has found that thanksgiving and positive thinking, even when not focused on God, change our brain's wiring and help us to experience trials differently. Even simply accepting difficult situations rather than constantly fighting them brings relief. When God is in the picture, shifting from our limited understanding to trusting His unlimited perspective can bring peace and hope.

This concept is very difficult at first and may not feel right or good. However, through making this change in focus, we can come to trust that God is still in control when things are not good. We do not have to be in control or to understand everything that's happening in order to be safe. We can remind ourselves that He has us in His hands and we can trust Him even in the midst of trials, uncertainties, and life not turning out as we desire.

Throughout Ecclesiastes, Solomon's statements about God point to our need to have a right understanding of who He is.

Some people think of God as a genie who is here to serve us or a coddling grandfather who overlooks our sins and spoils us by giving us all that we want. If this is who God is, then He is limited and of no real value to worship and serve. However, if God is beyond our making and understanding and outside our control, He is worthy to be served and worshiped. Thankfully, He is also good and loves us more than we can ever comprehend. But this does not mean that He will do what we want and make things work the way we want. Our satisfaction is not His primary interest.

Solomon speaks of God being beyond our understanding and our temporal universe. Ecclesiastes 11:5 (ESV) says, "As you do not know the way the spirit comes to the bones in the womb of a woman with child, so you do not know the work of God who makes everything." He speaks about our accountability to God. All things come from His hand Solomon says. God will be the one to judge how we lived our lives.

For some, this accountability can feel threatening, but for the Christian, it is a reminder of our dependence on Him. Accountability helps us to focus our lives on what really matters. Ultimately, we will be with Jesus in heaven one day and everything will make sense. In the meantime, we can take courage in the fact that God is in control and He will be the final judge. When things are unfair or seem unjust in this life, all will be made clear in the next.

The Teacher also addresses another misconception about suffering. He is clear that setbacks and suffering are not necessarily due to a person being unrighteous. Likewise, when things go well, they cannot always be attributed to our righteousness either. Stafford Wright said that Ecclesiastes reminds us that the purpose of life is not our own happiness or sorrow, and suggests that King Solomon points us to the fact that God has plans beyond that.[8]

At the end, the Teacher says in 12:13–14, "Now all has been heard; here is the conclusion of the matter: Fear God and keep his commandments for this is the duty of all mankind. For God will bring every deed into judgment, including every hidden thing, whether it is good or evil." Nonetheless, our focus is to be on trusting, regardless of how we interpret what is going on around us.

One afternoon Amanda arrived home from work intending to rush off to spend time with friends. When she got there, her mother was resting on the sofa and asked her to stay home and spend some time with her. Amanda thought her mother had been acting strange lately, and though she loved her dearly, at age twenty-four she had her own life to live and was not interested in having *another* heart-to-heart with her mom. Amanda's irritation got the best of her, and she snapped, telling her mother that she needed to "get her own life."

As she drove away she knew she had acted badly so she decided to come home earlier than planned to apologize and spend time with her mother. She admitted to herself, she had been out an awful lot lately and her mom was simply trying to show her love and care. She asked God for forgiveness as she pulled up to her friends' apartment and committed to making things right.

About two hours later, while Amanda was sharing nachos with her friends, she got a call from her dad. She almost didn't answer, thinking her dad would lecture her on being more respectful of her mom. Even so, to show God and herself that she had repented she answered.

To her surprise, her dad said her mom was on the way to the local hospital and wanted Amanda to meet him there immediately. Terrified, she raced to the hospital.

When she got there she found out her mom had had a major heart attack and was in critical condition. Amanda fell into her dad's arms and sobbed. She cried out to him and to God asking why God would let this happen to her mother. She was always so good, so loving, so tender. She rarely sinned and her sins were nothing compared to Amanda's. "This is *not* supposed to happen to godly people like my mom! Where is God? This is not fair," she lamented.

Then, Amanda's guilt for how she had talked to her mom surged up. *I repented to God on the drive. I thought that when we ask for forgiveness, He gives it immediately, so why is He doing this to me, to us?* Amanda implored God to have mercy and heal her mom.

While she was still pleading with Him, the doctor came out into the waiting room, walked over to her dad, and shook his head no. Amanda's ever-the-strong dad collapsed into a chair sobbing.

Discussion Questions

1. What are your presuppositions and expectations about how life should turn out for Christians?

2. Reflect on the Teacher's comments on our futile attempts to find satisfaction in life. How do they compare to your perception of what life should be like?

6

There Will Be Trouble

At this point, you might be thinking that surely Jesus saw suffering differently than the Teacher did. That the New Testament must give us reason to hope for restored justice and freedom from suffering. Well, Jesus doesn't give us a pass. The New Testament speaks of the Holy Spirit residing in us as being our hope *in the face of* difficult problems and suffering. It says the Holy Spirit helps us endure—and even overcome—whatever comes to us. In John chapter 14, Jesus promises that the Holy Spirit will come to believers and lets them know that He will be their comfort, their guide, and their peace. There is no promise that things will all work out for our ease, health, happiness, or success.

Yes, there are passages like Romans 8:28 (ESV): "And we know that for those who love God all things work together for good, for those who are called according to his purpose." However, we cannot isolate verses like these from the rest of Romans, the New Testament, or the Bible. The interpretation of passages like this must be viewed in light of the whole.

Jesus said in John 16:33, "In this world you will have trouble. But take heart! I have overcome the world." While some churches rarely proclaim this promise, Jesus Himself is making it clear that we cannot cling to the idea that since Jesus came and died for us, that things will be made easy, or easier. He did not say, trouble would only visit the unfaithful or those who continue to sin. He said "in this world," meaning that until we are with Him after death, we *will* have difficulties. But He also said that He has overcome the world.

Because of this we are no longer at the mercy of life continuing meaninglessly. Jesus' overcoming of the world means at minimum that all will be made right at the end of time, but more importantly, that He is with us through the Holy Spirit as we live in this world. Thus, we can tap into His perspective and His overcoming power.

In addition, the New Testament teaches that Christians may actually have a harder time than others because the world will hate us, just as they hated Jesus. While this has not been our common experience in our "Christian society," with the changing of our culture, we can expect to be increasingly disliked and despised for our beliefs and values.

We can learn much about how God uses suffering to shape His people from Jesus' relationship with Peter. Shortly before His own death, Jesus had predicted that His followers would face persecution (John 16:33); then He prayed for His immediate disciples, and all who would believe after them.

In John 17:15 (ESV), Jesus says to His Father, "I do not ask that you take them out of the world, but that you keep them from the evil one." He knew there would be trouble in this world for Christians so He prayed for protection from the evil one, *not* that we could somehow avoid it or be removed from it. He prays that we will remain united with God and focused on what He was focused on.

Yet, a few hours later during Jesus' trial, Peter gives into the temptation to protect himself and disowns Christ, instead of proclaiming allegiance to Jesus as he had so adamantly boasted he would. In Luke 22:31–34 (ESV), Jesus explained what was going on. He told Peter that the evil one had been given permission to sift Peter like wheat. The enemy wanted to take Peter down and God allowed him to try. The reality of Satan being allowed to torment and harm us may be somewhat jarring to consider.

Here is the key to understanding God's perspective: Jesus knew the plans He had for Peter and that Peter would be brought closer to Him if He allowed Peter to be tested. Peter did repent and it would appear that through this experience he likely reconsidered some of his ways. When he returned to Jesus he was humbled and more willing to surrender to Jesus' ways. Peter learned to depend on Him in all future service for Him and later, Jesus strengthened Peter.

Jesus treats us as He did Peter. He does not prevent adversity, but wants to use it to refine and strengthen us for more significant service. God did this in Paul's life as well. His life is an example of how God allows trials and pain but uses it to refine the believer and advance His Kingdom. Even so, He also provides for us and equips us to be able to endure.

Repeatedly, Paul spoke of Christians having the ability to endure or overcome troubles. For instance, Paul boldly declares in Romans 5:3–5 (ESV), "…we rejoice in our sufferings, knowing that suffering produces endurance, and endurance produces character, and character produces hope, and hope does not put us to shame, because God's love has been poured into our hearts through the Holy Spirit who has been given to us."

We can be thankful, not necessarily for the trial itself, but for what God will develop in us if we let Him. If we try to do this on our own, we may still develop endurance, but less character and hope. If we do this with God, the outcome will be our greater dependence and reliance on Him. When we allow our pain to draw us closer to God and to rely on Him more, we experience the love of God poured into us through the Holy Spirit; this helps us transcend the trials.

As mentioned, many have believed these passages about trials really only apply to persecution, but when we look further into Paul's life, we see that is not necessarily the case. Paul, who had been given surpassingly great revelations, was also given an ailment of some kind (which could have been either physical or emotional, we don't know) to keep him humble and focused on God. Paul explains this in 2 Corinthians 12:7–10 (ESV).

So to keep me from becoming conceited because of the surpassing greatness of the revelations, a thorn was given me in the flesh, a messenger of Satan to harass me, to keep me from becoming conceited. Three times I pleaded with the Lord about this, that it should leave me. But he said to me, "My grace is sufficient for you, for my power is made perfect in weakness." Therefore I will boast all the more gladly of my weaknesses, so that the power of Christ may rest upon me. For the sake of Christ, then, I am content with weaknesses, insults, hardships, persecutions, and calamities. For when I am weak, then I am strong.

It is not clear what ongoing problem Paul had. It is clear, though, that God gave Satan permission to harass Paul, and that He intended it for Paul's spiritual well-being and His own glory.

Paul had learned that he gained more through dependence on Christ than on his own strength. As a result, he could be content—not necessarily happy or excited—but content with his weakness and all kinds of trials because they bound him closer to God.

From a worldly perspective, nothing makes sense under the sun. But, from a heavenly perspective, all kinds of suffering and trials can be used to draw us closer to God, to build character and hope, and to make us more dependent on Him—for this is how we are essentially created to work best.

> We can be thankful, not necessarily for the trial itself, but for what God will develop in us if we let Him.

As I look back on the season of my life when I really didn't like myself, I vividly recall one night when I decided to turn things around. I had gone out, just to get away, and found myself driving aimlessly toward a work friend's neighborhood. I didn't know where she lived and I don't believe we had ever gotten together outside of work before. I stopped at a payphone to call her to see if I could come over. I knew she was a Christian, and I needed someone to talk to.

My life was a mess and I didn't know how to make it better. That night, after talking with her and her boyfriend, I recommitted my life to God and decided He must be able to do a better job of leading than I had. I shifted my understanding of God from being a distant savior to the active Lord. After that, things turned around in small ways, but it took six long years with many more challenges, trials, and deaths to self before I finally started liking myself.

Many things that pushed me beyond my natural abilities and way out of my comfort zone brought me closer to God. Now, when the Holy Spirit reminds me about the suffering I experienced when I tried to take control, I'm fairly adept at depending on God instead of myself. He used my pain to teach me to depend on Him more and in everything. God's way always works better.

James and his wife were struggling to reconnect after years of independent living. Barb loves the outdoors so James went with her on a hiking vacation in Maine where they could take day hikes in Acadia National Park. They enjoyed a week of exploring and hiking and agreed this was what they needed to kick-start their relationship.

A few weeks later, James came down with a terrible flu. He didn't heal as quickly as he usually did and even after he started to recover, some symptoms continued and at times he endured severe pain.

His energy plummeting, he was having trouble keeping his focus at work, so he finally saw a doctor. The doctor confirmed that a nasty flu had been keeping people down for weeks. He also explored the possibility of arthritis to explain some of James' severe joint pain. They discussed depression, as well, which can be common when men are approaching retirement. With James' work pressures and ongoing poor health, he could be moving into a mild situational depression.

After two more months of treatment, the symptoms did not improve. Work became too much and James retired at age sixty-seven. Staying was not worth the fight anymore.

At a doctor's appointment, he talked for the first time about his confusion over how this could have started right after his great hiking vacation with his wife. Privately, he had expected that God would bless his efforts to build his relationship with his wife. He certainly didn't expect poor health to be the result of such a wonderful trip.

The doctor had him review the timelines of his vacation and symptoms and sent James for a series of tests for Lyme disease. When the tests came back positive, James was relieved. He did everything he was asked to get his body and his life back, including multiple regimes of antibiotics. While most of his symptoms did improve over time, James continued to have muscle aches and fatigue. His doctor eventually told him that the Lyme disease was out of his system, but that a small portion of people continue to have these symptoms post-treatment. Not much could be done to heal post-treatment Lyme disease, as not enough research had been done on it.

With that discouraging news, James was dealing with an uncertain future. Again, he questioned the fairness of how this was all working out when he had always tried to live an upstanding life and now was trying to make the one area of his life that he hadn't focused on better.

Discussion Questions

1. When you face trials, what is your initial reaction toward the situation and toward God? Take some time to evaluate these reactions with curiosity (not judgment) in light of what you have been reading.

2. What new insights do you have after considering how Jesus and Paul both faced significant trials in their own lives, even when they remained fully devoted to God? How do their teachings challenge you?

3. If you have tried different responses to life's challenges, what difference do you find when you compare them? Which has worked best? Why do you think that is?

7

God's Inscrutable Ways

As we grapple with making sense of the idea that God thinks differently about our suffering than we do, it is helpful to explore further who He is. The idea that He might use suffering for our good may be new to you or something you are vaguely aware of in theory but have tried to ignore or have had little interest in exploring. If it goes against what you've learned in the culture around you and in your church, you may be asking, how can we trust a God like that? Or even, why would we want to trust a God like that? In this chapter we explore freshly who Scripture says God is and why we can trust Him, even when we cannot make sense of what is happening.

The Apostle Paul explores God's character and though he admits God's ways don't always make sense to us, he views God as still good in all of His ways. Paul declares in Romans 11:33 (ESV), "Oh, the depth of the riches and wisdom and knowledge of God! How unsearchable are his judgments and how inscrutable his ways!" Earlier in the chapter, he had been talking to the Gentiles about the mystery of God's justice and mercy. He used the example of how God would be willing to cut off some of His chosen people, the Jews, for their unfaithfulness and then accept the Gentiles, who were not His people. This is ultimate tough love and it goes against our current sensitivities. Without understanding the larger picture and His motivation, this just seems mean to us.

And yet, a little later on, Paul shows that in doing this, God wants to bring back those He had turned away. His love for them did not change; instead, He loves them enough to do whatever it takes to show them who He really is as well as their need for Him, so that He can restore them to Himself.

Some of us still use this kind of tough love to good effect. When a child is caught shoplifting, often the most loving thing to do is to allow them to face the police because it might help instill in them a fear of breaking the law. Rescuing the child might make us feel good in the short term, but may set them up for much greater suffering in the future.

This concept, of consequences teaching us how to live more effectively, is not limited to children. For instance, when addicts are allowed to face the consequences of their behaviors and life starts to fall apart, they are often motivated to get help and turn things around. People call this "hitting rock bottom". It tends to work because when we face the reality of our own limitations and depravity, we tend to seek help and change. When we do that, things can change significantly for the better.

Even if we have not had to deal with such extreme consequences, all of us have to live with the aftereffects of bad behavior. If we are married and repeatedly fail to let our spouses know we'll be late, our spouses will likely be upset and we will face conflict and strife until we can resolve the issue. If we continually goof off at work, we will be disciplined and could possibly lose our jobs, if we do not change. If we hurt our friends, they won't continue to return our calls and texts.

These consequences are not punishments but the natural outcome of our actions, unless someone steps in to rescue us. This is what Israel faced, for example, when God stepped back and allowed them to experience the natural results of their behaviors in hopes that they would recognize their actions and return to Him for reconciliation.

However, not all suffering is a direct response to or consequence of our actions. This is where understanding God's ways becomes challenging. So many people I see are wracked with guilt and pain for things that are not their fault. They question what they have done to deserve this punishment when in reality, their suffering is more a product of living in a broken world. Shootings, crimes, natural disasters, and terrible accidents happen to innocent people, not because they have done something wrong, but because of the underlying evil in our world. Many who are close to these victims can feel a strange sense of guilt for being spared what the others were not. Others beat themselves up for not somehow preventing this from happening, when in reality no one could have predicted or prevented it.

We do not understand God's wisdom because we do not understand Him or His greatness.[9] Delving into His greatness shows us that we cannot, in fact, understand God. His "infinite nature" encompasses all aspects of His being. He is limitless in all His ways, including space, time, understanding, wisdom, and power. God cannot be contained and He cannot be tamed. As humans, we struggle with this aspect of God, because our world and our reality are so limited.

Many of us prefer to focus on the loving side of God and how Jesus said in John 15:15 that we are no longer servants but friends of His because He has revealed God's plans to us. As Christians, we like that we have been given access to the "throne room" of God and we can go to Him personally without having to go through priests or religious leaders.

Others focus on passages where we can call God "Daddy," reflecting the deep intimacy that Jesus made available to us. In Romans 8:15, Paul says, "The Spirit you received does not make you slaves, so that you live in fear again; rather, the Spirit you received brought about your adoption to sonship. And by him we cry 'Abba, Father.'"

The problem is not that we believe and enjoy these passages. They are wonderful and fully accessible to us. The problem with focusing on these passages is that we neglect or ignore the fact of God's greatness. This side of His character is not negated by His love. In fact, we must keep both in balance to really know God for who He is.

Accepting God's greatness is one of the early steps we take in learning to surrender to Him. We accept that He is far greater than we imagine. Isaiah captures how hard it can be to come to terms with the immensity of God. In 40:13–14 he said, "Who can fathom the Spirit of the Lord, or instruct the LORD as his counselor? Whom did the Lord consult to enlighten him, and who taught him the right way? Who was it that taught him knowledge, or showed him the path of understanding?" This passage also reminds us of the balance in our relationship with God. When we do not understand what He is doing, it is not—and cannot be— because He is in the wrong. Therefore, our lack of understanding must derive from our limitations, not His.

Think of it this way—because His knowledge, understanding, and wisdom are not limited by time or space, He knows everything related to the past, present, and future. Therefore, God has a far more accurate perspective of our life and how it can work out than we ever could.

I know from experience that accepting God's directives can be challenging. Some of His prescribed ways do not immediately make sense to us and we want to try it our way, thinking we know better. I was in my early twenties when God asked the unthinkable of me. I had gotten myself into a relationship with a non-Christian man I loved dearly. He was adamantly not interested in becoming a Christian and did not see why that was a barrier to us marrying. For months I cried out to God to change his heart. I could not go forward without God's approval. You see, I kept remembering my earlier commitment to let God lead and the mess I had made of things when I didn't.

I also recalled a sense, on my first date with this man, that I should not date non-Christian men and that I had not listened. I had rebelliously put myself in this situation and now I wanted God to fix it so I could be in His will and keep what I wanted.

God did not relent. As I cried out in desperation, I felt God saying to me, "I cannot take you any further if you stay with this man. You have to choose—him or Me. If you choose Me, I will honor you." I can't tell you why I knew it was Him, but I did. I had to choose. Though God regularly brought his message back to my mind, it took time for me to be willing to accept His final say on the matter. Even though I felt certain He had spoken this to me, obeying His direction was excruciating.

For the next few months my boyfriend and I talked about how our differences in this area were too great, and we had to end it. He didn't agree, but I was firm, though I allowed my decision to be delayed over and over. I even went to my pastor to see if there was any "loop-hole" or way around what the Bible was saying. There wasn't.

After a number of joint commitments and delays, I finally said we had to stop. The day we finally broke it off, I called my sister, sobbing. She empathized with my pain and the sacrifice I was making. She comforted me, though nothing could take the pain away.

The next couple of months were very difficult. I knew I had made the right choice but my ex was not convinced. His sister-in-law found a pastor who would marry us, even with our differing faiths. He kept calling me, going between trying to convince me to reconsider and yelling at me for being so horrible. I loved him but my choice was God, no matter what. I finally had to put an end to the calls as well.

At the time, I believed that after I recovered from my loss, God would honor me by quickly bringing a good Christian man into my life for me to marry. But it took longer. It was over two years before I met anyone who even remotely showed any interest in me. For a short period, I connected with a man, but that quickly turned out to not be a fit.

Then—nothing for four more years. People would try to be encouraging, saying, "I don't understand why you are still single." That made me question what was wrong with me, though I know people did not intend it that way. I wrestled with God about my singleness and the possibility that I would never marry.

I finally got to the point of truly dying to that as well. I realized that God's honoring me related to other things, not to providing a husband, as I had assumed. Through that, I learned to lean on God and accept His ways as better than my own, even when it did not feel that way. He grew my faith to the point where I wanted what He wanted *even more* than I wanted what I wanted. I never fully decided I didn't want

> When we do not understand what He is doing, it is not—and cannot be—because He is in the wrong.

to be married, but I came to accept that if God figured that was better for me, then I wanted His plan instead of what I thought was best.

Once again, my way of pursuing what I had wanted led to deep pain when I had to let it go. I chose, going forward, to try to be obedient earlier in an effort to avoid unnecessary pain in the long run. Eventually, when I was in my early thirties, I married. Others who have made similar sacrifices of obedience never marry. Our only recourse against frustration, bitterness, and resentment is being willing to seek God's perspective.

Another early step in surrendering to God is accepting that His main interest is our character. Our individual pleasure, happiness, or comfort are of secondary importance to Him. He knows us so well that He can take into consideration what we think we know, as well as our reality, and what is actually best for us. He also considers every individual and works in all of us at the same time. Job 12:10 (ESV) declares, "In his hand is the life of every living thing and the breath of all mankind." And Isaiah 45:7 (ESV) says, "I form light and create darkness, I make well-being and create calamity, I am the LORD, who does all these things."

We may not like or readily accept His parameters but we can always bring our concerns and wrestling to Him. He has great patience with us and desires that we learn to rely on Him more, even in the surrendering to His ways. Wrestling things out with Him is about being honest and authentic with Him. When we don't agree with Him, He listens as He did to the psalmists who sang their laments. As we learn to be open with Him and "talk it out" with Him, He will help our wills to surrender to Him. Part of that journey is us becoming honest with ourselves in the process.

What is best in His estimation is always related to His will and plans for creation, plans for humanity to be reconciled to Him by our own choice. He created us to be in an intimate and dependent relationship with Him and to be conformed to His likeness. Paul says in Romans 8:29–30, "For those God foreknew he also predestined to be conformed to the image of his Son, that he might be the firstborn among many brothers and sisters. And those he predestined, he also called; those he called, he also justified; those he justified, he also glorified."

The gist of God's plan at creation is that He chose us to be in His family and to become like Him. He created everything so that He could have a family of believers who follow and reflect Him. Through our acceptance of the salvation process He restores us to right standing with Himself and He transforms us so we can share in His glory. This is an unheard-of privilege. However, in order to experience the fullness of this privilege, we must surrender fully to Him and His ways.

In Scripture, we see that our human knowledge and logic limit us in trying to understand what God thinks is best. God, for example, consistently chooses weaker, less educated, lower status people to carry out great tasks. Even His means of salvation is lunacy, according to human wisdom. Consider this explanation from 1 Corinthians 1:18, 25–31.

> For the message of the cross is foolishness to those who are perishing, but to us who are being saved it is the power of God … For the foolishness of God is wiser than human wisdom, and the weakness of God is stronger than human strength.

> Brothers and sisters, think of what you were when you were called. Not many of you were wise by human standards; not many were influential; not many were of noble birth. But God chose the foolish things of the world to shame the wise; God chose the weak things of the world to shame the strong. God chose the lowly things of this world and the despised things—and the things that are not—to nullify the things

that are, so that no one may boast before him. It is because of him that you are in Christ Jesus, who has become for us wisdom from God—that is, our righteousness, holiness and redemption. Therefore, as it is written: "Let the one who boasts boast in the Lord."

This passage also reminds us that we are completely dependent on Him for being in a relationship with Him at all. We cannot take credit for salvation, righteousness, holiness, and redemption. They are His idea, His plan, His orchestration, and His accomplishment. Our involvement is passive: we believe, receive, and submit to His ways.

Our role is to trust God. Proverbs 3:5–7 (ESV) states, "Trust in the LORD with all your heart, and do not lean on your own understanding. In all your ways acknowledge him, and he will make straight your paths. Be not wise in your own eyes; fear the LORD, and turn away from evil." Life works better for us when we recognize that God's ways are better and we accept that we will not understand how or why He works the way He does.

Chris' desire to reconnect with God and church continued to grow until he felt he couldn't put it off any longer. Life had to have purpose beyond work and raising kids. He loved his family, but his wife, Sandra, had all but checked out of their marriage. Her teaching schedule took more and more of her time, and she had never handled stress well. The whole house seemed on edge and Chris worried about what might happen to her.

Chris knew he needed to find peace and perspective for himself. He helped around the house to lighten the load for Sandra, but nothing seemed to be enough. They argued about church because she had no interest in going with him. Finally, he decided to go by himself.

Chris began attending a local church near his home. He enjoyed the worship and the friendliness of the people, but what got him most was the pastor's dynamic preaching. He was biblically grounded and did not shy from preaching about hard topics.

On Chris's second Sunday, Pastor Bill preached on marriage and submission. Chris was surprised they still preached on this, but what really caught his attention was the focus on how husbands were supposed to love their wives and be their spiritual protector. He had never heard that.

After the service he talked to the pastor about his wife's refusal to come to church with him. "How can I be her spiritual protector when she has no interest in God?" he asked. Bill empathetically listened and advised Chris to not pressure her. He urged him to love her in the ways that she needed and to privately pray for her.

From that day on, Chris prayed for her and his family daily, but felt like his prayers were not going any higher than the ceiling. When he met with Bill again, he talked to him about salvation and committing his life to being a follower of Jesus. Chris had never heard it put the way his pastor explained it. He had always thought being a Christian was about getting into heaven and then following the rules.

Pastor Bill talked about how God made it possible for Chris to have a personal relationship with Him. He helped Chris understand that through dying on the cross, Jesus had taken the punishment for his sins (behaviors and attitudes that separated him away from the righteousness of God). The pastor also helped Chris understand that Jesus' death allowed him to be connected with God as He had intended when He created us.

It made so much sense to him, so together they prayed and Chris received God's salvation and committed to seek after Him. As he prayed for his family that night, he felt a change. Instead of feeling like he was praying to an unknown being in the sky, he felt as though God was right there with him, listening to him. He also became eager to read his Bible and understand God more.

Over the following months he joined a Bible study to learn more about God. However, as he got closer to God, he seemed further from his wife. The more adamantly he prayed, the worse things got with Sandra. His study group empathized and yet still encouraged him to pray for her, while not pressuring her in any way.

Then, one night in early March he found his wife sobbing on the front steps of their home. Not much of what she said made sense, but he gathered that the children were safe and well. She was not. She had had a complete "meltdown" at work and could not return.

Chris listened and tried to comfort her by telling her everything was going to be okay. He gave her advice on what she could say and do when she went in the next day. Exasperated, she shouted, "You just don't get it! I can't go back there!" Confounded, he went with her to the doctor the next day. The doctor listened to Sandra's symptoms and life stressors and recommended a leave of absence for at least six to eight weeks, likely longer.

In the coming days, Chris tried to be supportive, but his own fear took over. *She could not leave work indefinitely; they needed her income. Where was the woman he knew and loved?*

This was not how Chris was expecting God to move. *What was He doing? Hadn't he given his life to God to lead it? Hadn't he been praying for Sandra daily?* He called Bill and the men in his study group. They all encouraged him that God was in control, and he could trust Him to get them through this. One person said, "You never know, this may have been what she needed for God to finally get her attention, and to help her learn to take better care of her own health and well-being."

They also said the situation was likely to move him into closer relationship with God. *But he was already getting closer to God, wasn't he? Was all of this necessary?* He asked each of them if there was a less painful way to get closer.

Discussion Questions

1. What do you think of the idea that God's ways and thoughts are so much higher, greater, and different from ours? How does that affect you? Why do you think that is?

2. How has your understanding of the greatness of God changed in light of what you have read? What impact does this make on how you understand who He is?

3. When have you struggled with your prayers not being answered the way you anticipated? How did you handle that?

8

What Exactly Does "Good" Mean, Anyway?

So many people ask, "How can a good God allow so much pain?" And yet, as we have seen earlier, pain is a natural part of this world. People also ask the question because of a general misunderstanding of what God's goodness is and of what He says is good for us. If we misunderstand and are influenced by current cultural sensitivities, we naturally have difficulty making sense of things that do not seem good to us.

As discussed earlier, some of us believe God's goodness means He will never allow us to feel pain or that He relates to us only as a coddling grandfather. In that case, when God does not respond the way we expect Him to, we are disillusioned and we begin to question God. "If He were really good, He would not allow these horrible things to happen to us," we reason.

This limited view of God's goodness cuts us off from experiencing His true goodness and care. Instead of understanding the fullness of God, we are left to deal with hardships in our own strength and limitations. We don't understand Him, so we don't trust Him. When we don't trust Him, we cannot turn to Him for comfort, support, or guidance. He feels unsafe.

However, when we can grasp who God really is and what He wants for us, we will realize that our good God is seeking to give us greater freedom and hope.

If we are to thrive as Christians, we need to build a sound view of God's character, one that reflects who He actually is. An accurate understanding of God impacts how we interact with Him, others, and ourselves. In particular, when we understand His goodness it allows us to trust Him more, even when still faced with uncertainties.

Beyond that, a solid understanding of God's good character affects our expectations and protects us from the hurt that comes from broken expectations.

Coming to understand the fullness of God's goodness allows us to run to Him when hardships come. We know we can trust Him to take care of us emotionally, even when it seems like He is not protecting us physically or situationally. We also find it easier to let Him help us change our perception of our situations to make them manageable.

Let's look at what Scripture and theology say about God's goodness, to build a more accurate picture. Christian theology can help us understand the goodness of God just as it did His greatness. Systematic theology suggests that God's goodness is made evident through the study of His relationship with His creation.[10] Thus, God's goodness is characterized by His moral qualities of moral purity, integrity, and love.

"Moral purity" relates to God being free of anything wicked or evil. God is holy—set apart, pure, and untainted. Exodus 15:11 says, "Who among the gods is like you, LORD? Who is like you— majestic in holiness, awesome in glory, working wonders?" His goodness is so far beyond us, He is worthy to be praised.

He is also unmarked by evil to the point that He cannot tolerate it in His presence. Like us, Habakkuk wrestled with this aspect of God's goodness saying, "Your eyes are too pure to look on evil; you cannot tolerate wrongdoing. Why then do you tolerate the treacherous? Why are you silent while the wicked swallow up those more righteous than themselves?" (Habakkuk 1:13). This is a hard concept because we do not always see God's intolerance for evil played out the way we think God would do things. Even so, in keeping with His character, God cannot abide by evil.

God is also righteous. His righteousness relates to His perfection and His way of acting in accordance with His moral law. The moral law, which He has given us, is based on His faultless character and nature. It was given so we would know what right and wrong are. Genesis 18:25 declares through this rhetorical question, "Will not the Judge of all the earth do right?"

At the same time, as Paul explains in Romans, while the law reveals God's righteousness, it also brings to light our sinfulness, which leads to death (and ultimate separation from God). He says:

> I would not have known what sin was had it not been for the law …I found that the very commandment that was intended to bring life actually brought death. For sin, seizing the opportunity afforded by the commandment, deceived me, and through the commandment put me to death (Romans 7:7–11).

Thus, justice is also a part of God's moral purity, in that, He always acts within, and requires conformity to, His perfect law. This has dire implications for us when we are left to rely on our own resources. Because His goodness is so far beyond us, our lack of holiness and righteousness excludes us from His presence. We may think this makes His goodness not good at all, but remember, His goodness does not depend on a relationship with us.

When we break God's law (and we often do, even in small ways), we sin and that requires God's justice. Sometimes that means correction. He also allows us to feel the consequences of our sins as a way of teaching us and inviting us to turn to Him more.

God's integrity also relates to absolute truth as God defines it. He is genuine, which means that all that He appears to be and claims to be is reliable. Further, everything is as He says, because he cannot lie or misrepresent the truth. This means that what we read in the Bible is true and cannot be not true. For instance, when

God promises to be with us always (Matthew 28:20), it means He is *always* with us even when we do not feel it. When He promises to be an ever-present help in times of trouble (Psalm 46:1), we can rely on this. I'm afraid He gets to define "help" though, so sometimes we need to ask Him to show us what He sees.

While He is all powerful and we might assume that He can do anything He wants, He cannot go against His own nature. This means God cannot lie or do evil. Although God's judgment as played out in the Old Testament often does not seem good to us, it was in full accordance with His moral purity and His integrity.

God's integrity includes His faithfulness. God always keeps His promises, proves Himself to be true, and does what He says He is going to do. In other words, we can trust God. When He says He is for us, He is for us (Romans 8:31). He is faithful to us and to all He has promised us.

Finally, God's love is an integral part of His good character. In fact, God can be defined as love, and His very nature embodies love. This kind of love includes His unselfish benevolence toward those He loves. He is always concerned for us and unselfishly gives of Himself for our sake. His love is not self-seeking but is directed toward us. He does not *need* us to return His love for Him in order for Him to continue to pour out His love toward us. This kind of love is not sentimental or biased in any way. It is "agape" love—unconditional and absolute.

He gives His love according to our need and His generosity, rather than because we deserve it. For example, when He offers salvation, He extends His love to us all, through grace that we do not merit; we are completely unworthy of it. Even when we are Christians, He continues to extend His love and mercy when we regularly sin and fall short. King David was considered a man after God's own heart (Acts 13:22) even though he committed most of his seemingly worst sins after he was in relationship with

> He does not *need* us to return His love for Him in order for Him to continue to pour out His love toward us.

God. God offers His mercy—His loving compassion—toward us because *we* desperately need it. His love is persistent and relentless.

In truth, it is because of His love that He withholds judgment. John 3:16 says, "For God so *loved* the world that he gave his one and only Son, that whoever believes in him shall not perish but have eternal life" (emphasis mine). Remember, part of His goodness is His justice that had to be met. Because He is love and He gave His Son to pay our penalty, we do not receive the punishment of death that Paul spoke of in Romans 7. After lamenting about how he is powerless to keep the law in his human strength, Paul declares the freedom that God gives us due to His extravagant love for us in Romans 8:1–4:

> Therefore, there is now no condemnation for those who are in Christ Jesus, because through Christ Jesus the law of the Spirit who gives life has set you free from the law of sin and death. For what the law was powerless to do because it was weakened by the flesh, God did by sending his own Son in the likeness of sinful flesh to be a sin offering. And so he condemned sin in the flesh, in order that the righteous requirement of the law might be fully met in us, who do not live according to the flesh but according to the Spirit.

What does this mean for us? It means that we can trust God and that we may need to ask Him to change our views and understanding of Him when they are not aligned with His true nature. This is not simply a mental agreement about who God is, but rather a deeper understanding and acknowledgment of who He really is. We can ask Him to help us to see things differently when we recognize that we may have misinterpreted Him or what has happened. It's an act of faith to acknowledge to ourselves that even if we don't understand what's happening or misunderstand God in general, He *is* love, trustworthy, and good.

We don't often question Him when He allows good things to happen to us. And we can trust that if He allows something that does not *feel* good, *His* being good means He intends good for us regardless of how we see things.

In Romans 8:28 Paul says, "And we know that in all things God works for the good of those who love him, who have been called according to his purpose." The often missed caveat is that God defines "good" here. Remember, God's definition of good as it relates to us still refers to what brings Him glory and is in line with His will. What is good for us is our being conformed to Christ's image—us changing to become more and more like Him in character and action.

He has a plan to bring good within all things *for those who love Him* and *are called according to His purpose*. Did you catch that? This promise is for Christians who love Him and who are called according to His purpose—our focus in this is to be on Him and His purpose, not the content of our situations. In everything He is working for our good but this does not mean that somehow all things magically become good in-and-of-themselves. Not at all. God is personal. He will be faithful and bring good (glory to Himself, fulfillment of His will, our becoming more like Christ) out of even the worst situations, for those who are focused on Him.

Having a sound view of God's goodness is not about life's *content* becoming good in ways *we* would like it to. There may be many good and even godly things you would like right now that God is not giving you. You may want a spouse to share your life with. You may want children and it isn't happening. You may want a good job so that you can support your family. These are not bad wants. However, when God seems to withhold them, He is looking to develop something better, something richer in us—if we are willing to see things from His perspective. He can bring hope, comfort, and healing and then grow us in ways that would not have been possible if we had not gone through that pain.

While I was in my first year of Bible college, a speaker talked about his missionary journeys in China, where he had met a man who had been imprisoned for years because of his Christian beliefs. What was so striking was that this once imprisoned man spoke of the richness of fellowship with other Christians in the rare times they would meet in the restrooms or the almost tangible closeness of God he felt when he was returned to his coffin-sized cell for hours on end. The missionary told us that this man teared up at missing that closeness with God since his release.

This is the God we serve! He can draw us so close that even horrendous experiences can become sweet with His closeness. In fact, the missionary noted that the Christians he was with in China were, and likely are to this day, praying that we in the West would experience persecution so that we could experience God in this way.

A look back to the start of the Church in the book of Acts reminds us that God used persecution to expand the Church from the confines of Jerusalem out into the rest of the Roman Empire. From the first believers, to the imprisonment of Paul, God used trials and pain to deepen relationships with Him and to accomplish His will on earth.

Unfortunately, many of us in the West miss the richness of God's goodness because we think that all we have to do is accept salvation to experience Him. Of course, initially receiving salvation is wonderful and many people do feel God's closeness then. But, if we stop seeking Him and investing in a daily relationship of dependence on Him, we lose the connection. Imagine being married and only talking to our spouse when we need them for something. And then when they don't come through as we expect, because we really don't know them, we are hurt and either take it personally or reject them for it.

We could have prevented this through daily conversations and intentional effort to really know one another. Then when our spouse does not do what we expect, we are able to consider their character and give them the benefit of the doubt regarding their intentions toward us. Relationship with God is the same. When we know His character and trust His goodness, we can lean into Him and believe through faith that even still, He is looking out for us.

One other argument against God's goodness needs to be addressed here. Many Christians wrestle with the question about what happens to "the other people," the ones who do not love Him, know Him, or seek Him. Doesn't He work good out for everyone on earth? Evidently, no. Wait, why not? How is God perfectly good if He lets people suffer and even go to hell? Good questions. They relate to the problem of evil and where sin came from in the first place.

Out of love, God created humans with free will, something we highly value and fight for today. In doing this, God had to create the *opportunity* for us to disobey Him, and thus to sin. For actual love to be returned, one must have the option to *not* love. For obedience to be actual obedience, the option to disobey must be available. And I am not only talking about the "big," obvious sins, I am talking about all sins, even the little, explainable sins. All disobedience ruptures our relationship with God.

> For actual love to be returned, one must have the option to *not* love.

However, we must remember that God also provided a solution to the issue of our sin and became the ultimate *victim of sin* when He took on the punishment for the sins of *every* human through dying on the cross. He didn't have to do that. The payment has been made for all, even if some choose not to receive it.

Even so, His design remains. He requires all people to *choose* to accept His free, undeserved gift and to love Him. He will not force His grace on those who do not want it. Of course, there are firm parameters to receiving this grace. It is offered only as all or nothing. We don't get to choose what we want and do not want from Him. When people choose not to accept Him, they are choosing to forgo His forgiveness and provision of ultimate goodness in all things. They choose to have none of Him.

It is the same for Christians on a lesser scale. When we accept His gift of salvation and put our eternity in His hands, we are secure, but He wants to do more. He wants to change us and free us from ourselves, so He continues to bring us around to seeing the areas in our lives that need His restoration.

We are like a house desperately needing renovations and Jesus, our master renovator, takes us to the next room requiring work. We can say no and He will not force His way in. However, He will keep bringing us back to *that* room until we are willing to address it. Being taken back to rooms we try to avoid is often painful and becomes more painful each time around. He's persistent, but it's for us to finally realize that the area needs to be restored. But He is gentle and patient through the process. Our lack of understanding is a reflection of our finiteness.

Linda had been estranged from her parents for years after they sided with the church instead of with her during her first divorce. Even when they finally did reconnect, the relationship remained strained because her parents wanted her to come back to the church. From Linda's perspective, her life was better off without all of that. But now, with her partner John becoming a Christian, she is finding it difficult to get away from God.

A few years ago, her father had passed away and now her mother, Helen, lives on her own in Linda's childhood home. Since then, Linda and her mother have become closer, though Linda still resists any conversations about God. Her mother no longer presses her on this and, when Linda's honest with herself, she can admit that it has been years since they'd talked about church. Her mother has also become more loving. This began about fifteen years ago when something changed with her parents, and they became more loving and accepting of each other and her.

Because she really loved John, and feared a break-up, Linda asked her mother about what changed. As they sat on the porch that July afternoon, Helen grew quiet for a moment, and then said she had been praying for this day to come for so long. While in the past that would have repelled Linda, the love and tenderness in her mother's eyes held her. Helen surprised Linda by first apologizing for what she had had to endure growing up. She confessed her own shortfalls and those of her husband. She also apologized for how they had behaved during Linda's two failed marriages and for the pressure they had put on her.

Linda hadn't realized how much she had longed for that until she heard her mother's heartfelt remorse. She accepted her apologies and then asked again what had happened to bring the change.

Helen shared how things had become so terrible she was planning on leaving her own marriage. But, when Linda's father had his first round with cancer, she couldn't do it. Instead, she turned to God and began praying in ways she never had before. Her faith moved from religion to dependence on a personal God who saw her.

Helen's husband continued to be cantankerous as the cancer battled him, and he had taken it out on her. However, in surrendering to God's call to love Him first, she found a surprising hope. As Helen had poured over her Bible and Christian books on suffering, she found a God who loved and valued her, even if her husband didn't. She realized she didn't have to fight for her worth or prove that she deserved better. God *saw* her. He loved her. She was enough, just as she was.

She shared that as she stopped needing her husband to appreciate her and meet her needs, he began to see the change in her. Slowly, he too softened, and one night when he was in great pain after radiation, he talked about his own fears. They talked for hours and decided they would seek after God together—not the God of religion and rules, but the God who saw and loved them both.

Through their times with God, they confessed and forgave each other for all the ways they had mistreated each other. They read books on relationships and how to love one another better, and they relied on God when the other was not keeping up their side of the bargain. "God changed us when we stopped focusing on how *we* thought life should be, when we stopped trying to *do* religion the way we thought it should be done, and when we surrendered to *His* ways," she concluded.

Linda was stunned. This did not sound like the Bible thumping, judgmental, rule-requiring woman she had known. Her mom had talked a lot about God and what she had learned from Him and the Bible in a way that Linda could relate to. She was still skeptical and leery, but she had to admit, her mom was different.

Discussion Questions

1. How has your understanding of the goodness of God changed in light of what you have read? How does this affect how you understand who He is?

2. How do you define "good" in relation to how God interacts with you and with the world now?

3. How might God being good affect how you interpret the challenges in your life?

9

What's Counting the Cost About?

As we continue making our way across the valley floor, we have reached a place of reorientation. We have been trying to understand God's nature and perspective so we can learn to trust Him more in our journey of dying to self. Here, let's make a slight shift in focus to "count the cost" of moving ahead. By taking time now to understand, we will have realistic expectations and not be deterred when we face a seemingly impossible sacrifice. This will also allow us to more fully embrace the value of dying to self.

Being able to live the life He created us to live means we must be willing to be conformed to Him. Paul explains how this happens in Romans 12:2: "Do not conform to the patterns of this world, but be transformed by the renewing of your mind." Over time, this awakening of our minds will allow us to adopt God's perspective and live more easily by His values. As we do this, we gain wisdom and understanding that helps us to transcend problems and remain rooted in the knowledge of God's love and provision for us. It also frees us to live more joyfully because we are no longer striving and fretting about what we *should* be doing. Instead, we can confidently "be," knowing God is guiding our steps and paths.

However, before we can move on, we must explore what this surrender really costs us. You see, counting the cost is not only about what we must give up, but also what we will receive in return if we do. This is an evaluation of whether it is worth making the sacrifice God is requiring of us and it is about fully understanding what that sacrifice actually entails. Here we look at Jesus' teaching on living His way and of becoming more like God.

Again, we are facing some challenging concepts. You may start to examine dying to self and wonder if the promised freedom is worth it. You might feel resistance, irritation, or even anger. I have heard these reactions from others, who have said, "God would not require this." Or, "I don't need or want Him to take that much control over my life."

If you start to feel that way as you navigate this chapter, hold on to what we have learned—God is good and cannot not be good. His ways are not our ways and we cannot understand His wisdom from a human perspective. Yet, we can trust that His ways are good and will bring the very best results for us.

In the latter portion of the fourteenth chapter of Luke, Jesus teaches His audience what is required to be His disciples and prepares them, and us, to make informed decisions as we consider this role. Just a point of clarification, these teachings are not a requirement of salvation. They are about living a life beyond merely getting into heaven. This is about abundant life in the now. But, the cost for this kind of life is great.

Jesus bookends His teaching with two radical and all-encompassing statements about this cost. In Luke 14:26–27, He says, "If anyone comes to me and does not hate father and mother, wife and children, brothers and sisters—yes, even their own life—such a person cannot be my disciple." In verse 33, Jesus concludes by boldly declaring "those of you who do not give up everything you have cannot be my disciples." He is talking about our loyalty to Him, but more so, about our priorities.

You may be thinking, hold on, this does *not* sound like abundant life at any time! He wants us to *hate* everyone that is important to us: our parents, our siblings, our spouses, our children, and even our own lives? And, He wants us to give up everything we have? And, we cannot be His disciples unless we do this?

Before you turn away, or throw this book, letʼs pause. We will navigate this terrain together. Between these two declarations, Jesus provides two powerful examples of what counting the cost looked like in His cultural context. We will explore these two stories along with two found elsewhere to bring clarity to these radical requirements.

> His ways are not our ways and we cannot understand His wisdom from a human perspective.

The first story is of a wise builder who inventories his resources before beginning a major building project. He prepares an estimate of the project costs, looks at his resources, and then evaluates whether it is worth taking on the project. The building may be wonderful in the blueprints, but if the resources are not there to complete it, it is wise not to take on the project.

The second story is of a king who compares his military strength to that of an attacking army before sending his troops into battle. The kingʼs options are to fight to protect the kingdom or to send a delegate to see if a peace treaty can be arranged. In both cases loss will be incurred. The king must weigh what course of action will be most advantageous for his people.

In both stories, the individuals counted the cost of a possible course of action by evaluating the best routes to achieve their goals and determined whether it was worth the expense. The challenge with this idea of counting the cost is that we often do not realize the value of what we are holding so tightly to in comparison to what we will receive if we let it go. For many people, it feels like God is asking us to give up things of great value without any guarantee of receiving equal or greater value in return.

For instance, I often hear about fears of giving over control to God because people do not know or trust what God will expect of them. They fear He may send them to foreign lands to be missionaries or He may make them stay in an uncomfortable living situation or give up something they really do not want to let go of like their next dream purchase. God rarely gives us specifics of the other side of the deal and that makes most of us very uncomfortable, indeed.

Let's bring in two of Jesus' parables to add further clarity to the value of what Jesus is offering us. In them, He talks about the kingdom of heaven, which is not only something we'll enjoy when we die, but is what He offers in the now as we die to self and give Him control. He does not hold this back until we die, He is offering us part of heaven in the now, our current life. He is saying that the kingdom is so valuable that it is worth us selling or giving up everything we hold dear to have this incredible treasure.

The first story is the parable of the hidden treasure in Matthew 13:44: "The kingdom of heaven is like treasure hidden in a field. When a man found it, he hid it again, and then in his joy went and sold all he had and bought that field." This man found something of such immense worth that when he counted the cost, he decided to sell all he had in order to gain this treasure. By his estimation the found treasure was worth far more than what he actually had.

The second parable, which is in Matthew 13:45–46, is that of a pearl merchant: "Again, the kingdom of heaven is like a merchant looking for fine pearls. When he found one of great value, he went away and sold everything he had and bought it." The merchant found a treasure of so much value that, after comparing the cost of acquiring the new pearl to the value of all the others he had, he decided it was worth selling everything to have the one pearl.

Are you starting to catch a glimpse of it?

Let's look back at Luke 14:26–27 to explore how living in the kingdom of heaven relates to hating our loved ones and our lives. I agree—"hate" is a challenging word. I do not believe that Jesus is asking us to actually feel hate or behave in a hateful way toward our loved ones or ourselves. Nor is Jesus suggesting that our loved ones are bad or negative. That would go against His character. Since Jesus cannot contradict Himself, let's look deeper.

Rather, He requires that we put our loyalties with Him first because we cannot be focused on, or devoted to, both. We see how serious this is today when people of some religions decide to become Christians. By choosing Christ, they accept that they will be fully cut off from their loved ones. This is a big sacrifice.

Most of us do not face that kind of choice. Instead, the choice could be making time to spend in prayer or reading our Bible when others in our family want us to do something with them. In some families you may be ridiculed or put down for spending time with God. Or, the choice could be making it a priority to go to church instead of relaxing on Sunday mornings, going to sporting events, or doing other things that loved ones want you to do weekly and that would interfere with regular church attendance. (I say "regular" because God is not legalistic and I don't want anyone thinking if you miss a worship service or two that you cannot be His disciple—that is simply not the case). Your choices to follow Jesus may cause conflict with your family, but Jesus is saying we need to make Him the priority over other things including the contrary opinions of loved ones.

If we cling to our family or their contrary values and expectations, we can never obtain the treasure that is available should we let go of them. If we put all of our energy and love into what seem to be the good things and are not willing to release them, even if God is asking, then we are in danger. God is not asking us to make hard choices for no reason and He is not mean-spirited. If He is asking us to let go and make Him our priority, then He has something *better* planned. Giving Him priority is one of the ways that our minds are renewed. Though it sounds crazy at times, seeing life from His perspective brings us more security, value, and hope than clinging to what we think we know does.

Dear friends of mine recently moved across the country because they believe God is calling them there for a season. They battled God at first because they had grown up here, gone to one church, and had family roots and friendships that ran deep in this area. What God was asking my friend's husband to do, he could have done locally. Even so, my friend also felt like God was the one asking them to move.

At first she was angry with God and fearful about leaving all that she had known to start fresh with no real connections. It took time to wrestle, vent, pray, and cry out to God before she came to the place of surrender. She realized that no matter what, she wants His closeness even more than she wants the closeness of the loved ones she would leave behind. Obedience to God was the only way. As soon as she gave in, she felt peace and hope about the move. While it has still been very hard in some ways, she rests in the assurance that God is with her and He has good plans for her and her family in this new place.

When we release what seems so necessary to our well-being, so precious, we shift our devotion so completely to Jesus that it seems as though we hate the things we were once devoted to. It becomes clear that *nothing* is worth clinging to in light of what is being offered—God Himself. *Do you see it?*

When we love ourselves, or anyone, or anything, more than God, we forfeit the riches He has for us. He wants to give them to us, but lets us make choices. Some are more damaging than others. Poor choices not only have consequences in us missing out on God's riches, but also in pain and suffering or emptiness and regret, which are a natural result of our decision. There is a disturbing ad on TV to discourage people from texting while driving. A young man is driving and looks down to read a text. Another car hits him and he is jarred. The camera flips to this same man in a hospital room. He appears to be paralyzed and is wearing a brace around his neck. This ad makes its point about poor decisions starkly.

We can also face consequences on a spiritual level. One pastor spoke of a devoted Christian family who loved the Lord but allowed their young son to put his priority in sports rather than on worshiping in church on Sundays. Having children in sports and encouraging them to excel is good for them. The young man excelled and had success in his sport, but now, in his thirties he has retired from sports and has a regular job. The spiritual consequence is that he does not know the Lord and has no interest in God. Though he experienced worldly success, it cost him the riches of God's kingdom.

Like you, I know making such choices is usually tough, even when we accept that God is good and trustworthy. When I had just started full-time psychotherapy, the psychologist I worked for and I started doing assessments to supplement our income. They were lucrative and valuable to our clients; however, it was not my passion or strength. Over time that part of the business grew faster than my practice and more than half of my practice was assessments. I began having to turn away therapy clients because my schedule was full. This was not what God had called me to and I knew it. However, letting that side of the business go would significantly impact my bottom line.

As I wrestled with this and talked to my husband about it, he was less than enthusiastic about me making a change. Even so, I truly believed God was again pushing me to trust Him. I did. Ten years later, I still do not make what I made in those early years. This was a major financial sacrifice but the blessings I have received from seeing many more clients healed and drawn closer to God has been more than worth it for me.

Every time we make a choice to submit what we want to God, we grow and become more of what He created us to be in the first place. The peace and joy that come on the other side of surrender and submission are worth it. Some of you are being required to remain single; some are releasing your intense desire for children. Some of you feel paralyzed as you watch your children make bad life choices and struggle to not allow that pain to become a block between you and God. Some of you are desperately seeking work and cannot find anything in the field you are trained in. Still others are in unhappy marriages and cannot seem to get your spouses to want to change. I recognize that dying to and letting go in situations like these is excruciating. How can we let go of the need to control these situations and be open to something different?

If you are finding it hard to accept that God's perspective is far better, that is natural because we don't understand something until we experience it. Perhaps this illustration, which I use with my clients, will normalize the experience.

Imagine meeting someone who has never seen or tasted chocolate. You present them with a dark brown solid square. It does not look like something they would want to put in their mouth. Even as we describe the wonderful mix of bitterness and sweetness, they remain skeptical. Did you know chocolate is said to have a multitude of differing flavors within it for those who take the time to savor it?[11] Further, it does not look like it would melt with a smooth texture on the tongue and leave a delightful after-taste. How can we do it justice with our descriptions? They will never really get it until they taste it for themselves. Will they stay "safe" or try a piece of chocolate?

When God asks us to surrender control, will we try to stay safe or take the needed steps? What I am talking about is releasing control to Jesus and trusting that He *is* in the process. Even if the situation does not turn out the way we desire, focusing on trusting Him will allow us to navigate the experience differently, with more hope and security.

The process of surrender is a shift of the will and a choosing to let go of what we are holding onto. However, it is more than simply a cognitive process. Our thoughts are involved but we cannot make this shift until something deeper at a core emotional level accepts and agrees; a heart shift, if you will. That is where the process gets a bit fuzzy. This is more than a mental ascent, this requires an internal release as well. That is where we need God's assistance. The process can first be an all-encompassing surrender to Him, followed by calls to trust Him in specifics.

My prayer is that all who walk this trail with me would *lean in* to surrender rather than saying no at this point. We can trust that God will give us insights, that He will act with the right timing, give us courage, and change our perspective. If we ask Him to, the Holy Spirit will work with us so we can press on.

It helps to realize that when it comes to surrender, we are in an interactive wrestling match with God and yet He is on our side. We are wrestling with Him against ourselves and the parts of us that hold us back from receiving the fullness He has for us. He will help us to finally give over our hopes, dreams, and wants so that He can give us something *better*.

Press in. It is worth the battle. When you genuinely let go of having life your way and release control to Him, you will gain deep freedom. You will know that you will be okay, no matter what the outcome.

Late in October, Jen was preparing to work her final week at the company she had been with for the last three years. With the colored leaves falling outside, she braced herself for the dead of winter she knew was coming in her spirit. Over the past few months no new work prospects had come up. She would be given a fair severance package, but it would not last long with her mortgage payments and bills. *If only I were not alone in this, things wouldn't look so bleak*, she lamented.

Jen was exhausted from the long hours. She regularly questioned herself on why she was working so hard when the company did not care about her. Even so, her strong work ethic would not let her slack off, even now. Night after night she cried out to God: *Why are You making things so hard on me. What more could I do to earn Your approval?* With no apparent response, she came to believe there was something fundamentally wrong with her. He seemed to be moving in everyone else's life, and she was doing all she knew to do. Clearly the problem must be deep within her.

When she was honest with herself, she recognized she had never felt like she measured up. Even with her MBA, she often felt like a fraud who could be exposed as a failure. She felt that this lay off and having no job in sight further proved it. *At this stage, things were* supposed *to be so different.*

Added to this, she had not really dated much at all in her almost forty years. The pain of not having a husband and family haunted her. Others who seemed less put together had found partners long ago.

Jen still attended church and went through the motions of serving, but was beginning to wonder if God really cared for her. *What is the point of all of this? It just isn't going to work for me no matter what I do!* In her despair she reasoned that what she was asking for was not that big of a deal, that it would not be hard for God to give them to her. After all, He had for others.

Knowing she was not doing well, she sought out Sharon, a Christian counselor, to help her deal with the pain of her job loss and to figure out what to do. To her surprise, they ended up focusing more on her relationship with God and her longing for a family more than on her work situation. Sharon helped her understand that her body/emotions know what needs to be worked on first, and that it was okay to focus on this. Although Jen had said her concern was work related, she repeatedly brought up other issues that held pain, an indication to Sharon that that was where they needed to focus first. Clearly, this longing was actually causing the most distress. Jen liked Sharon and built a safe relationship with her.

One day, when Jen was again lamenting her lack of romantic prospects, Sharon challenged her to release these dreams to God. She assured her that it was not because they were bad dreams; in fact, they were good ones. But they were getting in the way of something more that God had for her. It seemed so cruel to Jen. She moaned, *Why would God take even my dreams for this away? Wasn't it enough that He had not let me have them in reality?*

As they talked, Sharon explained the freedom that comes through dying to self and to her hard-held desires for her life. This resonated with Jen, but when she left the office and tried to put this into practice, it was a battle. Though she believed Sharon was right, she still resisted this being the only way. Anger rose in her. *Why is this required? How come others are able to have this life and I am forced to give it up? This is not fair!*

At the same time, she did not want to lose God, and deep down she longed to believe He had a good plan for her if she let go. She really wanted the connection and peace Sharon had described. Then she'd flip back, repeating to herself that she also really wanted a family. So back and forth she wrestled.

Discussion Questions

1. As you think of counting the cost of following Jesus, how has looking at what you could possibly gain affected you? How do you view what you might lose?

2. How do you feel about releasing control of the things you hold dear into God's hands? What fears arise?

3. What things are you holding tightly to but know God is asking you to let go of? How has this chapter affected that battle for you?

10 | Impossible "Shoulds" or Unexpected Possibilities?

Still in the thick of the valley, we continue our search for beauty and hope in the midst of dying to self. So far we have come to see that God is good, and yet He is entirely beyond us in every way. We are to count the cost and seek to choose Him and His Kingdom and live by His perspective above all else. We must depend on the Holy Spirit to help us understand how God works in our lives.

When we become aligned with God, decisions and actions that seemed impossible shift to being possible. In addition, what we thought were obligations and pressure-filled "shoulds" become invitations to activities we are able to do and even want to do. We end up experiencing life in the now in new ways.

Impossible "Shoulds" Become Conceivable "Coulds"

So often we approach our Christian faith as though we are living out of a paradigm of religious rules and regulations. We focus on our behavior, trying to do all that the Bible describes and commands, like going to church, tithing, praying, reading our Bibles, serving, and so on. These are all good, but if we are doing them for any reason other than as a *response* to living in partnership with God, these activities become religious obligations instead of avenues to connect with God.

Before Jesus came, those seeking to know and be in relationship with God seemed limited to doing so in their own strength by keeping the law God had given via Moses. This led to impossible religious standards and legalism, but not freedom. Jesus said in Luke 4:17–21 that He came to set the captives free. This freedom comes because Jesus perfectly fulfilled the law for us, as He states in Matthew 5:17. With His freedom, we can partner with the Holy Spirit to live up to what God requires instead of us trying to do that to win or appease Him.

However, we may wonder about that freedom when we look at some of Jesus' direct teachings on how we are to live. Some of them challenge us to even higher standards than in the Old Testament law. That does not seem like the freedom Jesus promised. So, once again we must look deeper to understand how Jesus' teaching is to be interpreted in light of the freedom He promises.

Let's begin by looking at one of Jesus' most challenging standards. In Matthew 5:20 He said, "For I tell you that unless your righteousness surpasses that of the Pharisees and the teachers of the law, you will certainly not enter the kingdom of heaven." These were the people who knew the law the most and thus were most likely to be able to follow it. I don't know about you, but I know I cannot perfectly follow all of the requirements given in the law. So, to understand what He meant, we start from the perspective that since Jesus cannot contradict Himself, He could not have intended to place a more difficult requirement on us than what was in the law. Something else must have been going on.

From Matthew 5:20 on, Jesus explained to His audience that the real intent of the law was not to have us keep the various rules and regulations, but for us to have an inner change of attitude and thinking. For instance, the heart of "do not murder" is not holding onto anger and judgment of others. The heart of not committing adultery is to keep our mind pure and protect ourselves from even allowing our eyes and our minds to entertain such thoughts. We are not to get even with others who have wronged us even when it seems just, and loving our enemies is about going beyond what is natural for us and learning to extend undeserving grace and love the way Jesus does.

Unfortunately, the Pharisees missed the heart of the matter and focused on their actions. Jesus was hard on them because they had studied the law and were supposed to understand God's intent, not to focus on the things that could never bring real righteousness. With that thinking, they could not carry out their responsibility to help others understand that what God wants most is heart change.

Jesus also used the Matthew 5 passages to illustrate that we cannot live up to His calling to be holy, in our own strength. We cannot become righteous through performance. Sadly, some Christians count on their actions to win them favor with God and lose out on the freedom and joy that comes from a close relationship with God. They run the risk of ending up discouraged and disillusioned because their striving never seems to gain them the peace they long for. Further, when bad things happen, they question God's goodness because they feel He is not holding up His end of the bargain—a bargain He never actually agreed to.

Even if we go to church every week and to a mid-week service, honor our parents, do not murder, lust, steal, covet, swear, or speak negatively about other people, or give all of our time, energy, and money to serving, it is not enough. Nothing in our power can create the righteousness that God requires. When God set the standards in the law, He knew that the Israelites could not meet them. In fact, He gave us the law to make His people aware of their need for Him. Paul, in Romans 7:7–12, points out that the law actually increased our sin by making us aware of it. Thus, instead of leading to life and freedom, the law led to death. However, Jesus is clear that the law is still holy and that we are to follow the moral standards set out in the law (the rituals and sacrificial law was completely fulfilled by Jesus and is no longer required for us).

So how has He made freedom possible? The key is that He has given us His own resources so we can live up to His moral standards. In *The Divine Conspiracy*, Dallas Willard said, "[Jesus] knew that we cannot keep the law by trying to keep the law. To succeed in keeping the law, one must aim at something other and something more. One must aim to become the *kind of person* from whom the deeds of the law naturally flow."

God is not as interested in us doing the right things as an end in themselves as He is in the inner change that is essential to us living according to His standards. That is why Jesus said our righteousness needs to be beyond that of the Pharisees. They had missed the heart aspect, thus rendering themselves and their followers powerless to do what was required.

Most of us have actions and attitudes that God wants to change. It could be about not reading our Bible or reading it by rote, not praying enough, not serving at our church, or more subtly, it could be about not loving one another, having self-control, or patience. When we try to do these things because we know we should, we have trouble maintaining the pace. And, even if we do, if it is simply so we can say we are behaving rightly, our activities do not have the same value to God as they would if real heart change had been the motivator. He wants our hearts and our devotion, not our behaviors for behavior sake.

Any time I have tried to read the Bible because I thought I *should*, I often closed it feeling frustrated or guilty. By contrast, when I have asked Him to make me want to read His Word, I felt good about having spent the time with Him, even when I didn't get a lot out of it. There doesn't need to be *results* every time we do this. God values our relationship *with* Him far more than our activities performed *for* Him.

Paul used himself as an example of how God values devotion and relationship more than religious zeal played out in activities. Pre-conversion, he had been a determined and highly effective Pharisee. In Philippians 3:5–6, he lists his stellar credentials to show why he had grounds to have "confidence in the flesh." And yet, he considered them of no worth; after his conversion experience with the true Lord Jesus, he considered them as "loss" compared to the "surpassing greatness of knowing Jesus" (Philippians 3:7–8). Paul could obey and submit to Jesus because God had changed him from the inside, and Paul's reason for following the law changed entirely. He did it because he loved Jesus and knew how much he was loved by Him.

It is the same for us. The only way we can live in a way that pleases God is to allow God to change us into someone who is *able* to act righteously naturally out of our devotion to Him, not out of obligation. When we let God change us, the "should" of living by God's standards change to a "can." Further, God changes our thinking so that what we are doing becomes less of the focus. Rather, we want a real encounter with God. The activities of obedience flow out of us naturally, with less effort, as we focus on drawing closer to Jesus. No more striving or pressure!

So No One Can Boast

Many of us want to receive the credit for our actions and the accolades now, but Jesus wants something better for us. Looking further into the Sermon on the Mount, we find in chapter 6 of Matthew that Jesus addressed a temptation we face in doing good. He taught that living out our righteousness is not intended to be an opportunity to draw attention to ourselves. Rather, Jesus intends any "reward" (v. 18) to be received in private. As a result, we are to give and pray in secret, and when we fast, to not change our appearance so others know what we are doing.

This does not mean we are to never let anyone see or know what we are doing; otherwise we could not do public service. Again, it is a matter of the heart. If we are giving so that others will notice and think highly of us, it is of no value to God. He says when we do that, we have received our reward in full. There will be no further reward waiting for us in heaven. This is the same for prayer and fasting or worship leading or organizing public events. We are not to use anything for our own glory and recognition. At the same time, we can know God is not taking us for granted but preparing a reward for us in secret that will be *greater* than that received in public.

Jesus' teaching on not seeking public recognition flows naturally from His warning to "store up ... treasures in heaven" (v. 19). The imagery that comes to mind is that of an investment bank account that gains interest. Doing things for worldly gain provides minimal returns. Doing things with a heavenly focus leads to high returns in heaven. Yes, this means delayed gratification, but as with most things, when we wait for something, the results are much sweeter.

Once again, our focus is not on the acts or on ourselves, but on God and serving Him. He wants to be involved. He is the one who invites and empowers us. This is about partnership *with* Him, not doing *for* Him. Oswald Chambers in *My Utmost for His Highest* says it this way: "It is the work that God does through us that counts, not what we do for Him."

We work with Him and thus, the results belong to Him and not us. He gets the glory, not us. In turn, He shares *His* glory and reward. His are better!

As we seek Him more, we no longer feel the weight of "should" or the pressure to succeed. Giving, praying, fasting, and serving in any capacity become things we do in relationship *with* God, instead of tools to gain acceptance from others or to win brownie points with Him. *Everything is about relationship with God.*

> The activities of obedience flow out of us naturally, with less effort, as we focus on drawing closer to Jesus.

Oswald Chambers describes the influence of this relationship on the way we pray. He says, "If the Son of God is formed in us... He will press forward in front of our common sense and change our attitude to the things about which we pray." In this partnership with God, we are able to pray the prayers He has for us instead of only those that fit within our common sense. This is a real change. It is not us trying to pray as He would, we simply do so as a result of His work in us.

We respond to His initiation, not in an effort to please or win His affection or acceptance. The pressure is off us. All of life is all about Him.

Relinquishing Control

As Jesus continues His sermon, He leans in to address another block to being in a strong relationship with Him—our efforts to have control and to provide for ourselves. We want the glory of self-sufficiency and Jesus cautions us about this.

He talks about our "treasures" (v. 19) and this could be anything that we value and put ahead of God, such as money, affirmation, family, sex, power, achievement, and status. If money drives us and our treasure is in what we can accomplish and gain in this life, we are in danger of missing *Him*, and that includes how well we can survive on a low income. Jesus, instead, encourages us to put all of our focus on partnering with Him in all things. Then we will have more peace.

Starting in verse 25, Jesus addresses an attitude that can come between us and Him—worry. In our rushed and busy world that stresses self-sufficiency, we worry that we will not be able to perform well enough, that people will judge us, that we will lose our jobs, that we will not have enough, that we are not good enough, that we will fail, that we will be alone.

When we trust and rely on God, we *do not have to* worry. True, learning to release our concerns to Jesus can be a challenge, especially for those prone to worry, but Jesus did not want to make us feel badly about our worry. He is revealing a better way.

As a psychotherapist, my income is entirely based on the clients I see. When there are no clients, I have no income. Throughout the years I have faced the ebbs and flows of normal practice. In the slow times of the early years, I would put pressure on myself and feel stressed. Yet, I knew I could not make people come to see me. And in honesty, there are some ethical issues with focusing on this too much in my profession.

So I had the choice of releasing my worry and trusting God to provide in His timing or allowing myself to be robbed of the rest I could be getting in the down times. I have now learned to be okay and even thankful for the slow periods, knowing the busy times will come again. The freedom is so much easier to live with.

Through trusting in God and allowing Him to work things out in His way, we can have peace even in the midst of difficulties. We can trust God with our future because we *know* He is good. No matter what, we *are* secure in Him. When we are trusting and relying on God, He helps us to see our circumstances differently so that we can navigate through them and be okay.

After months of wrestling with God, Jen was exhausted. She had gone back to reading her Bible regularly and listening to as many sermons as she could, through her church and the Internet. She was doing everything in her power to be the good Christian she thought she had to be, in hopes that God would see she was making an effort.

Then one night, while reading the Sermon on the Mount, she realized that what Jesus was calling for was actually impossible. She prayed and asked God to show her how anyone could live this way. She began to see that she had been missing something all this time. *Perhaps this is why things haven't worked out*, she thought. As she looked deeper and read a few commentaries, she realized this was the surrender Sharon had been talking about.

She was not supposed to be able live God's way in her own strength. She needed God to change her heart and equip her from the inside. For a moment, that felt freeing and then it occurred to her that she had no idea how to let God change her. Again, she felt lost.

In her next appointment with Sharon, she brought this up. Sharon admitted this is hard for most people. "The steps are not as concrete as most of us would like" she explained. "Instead, it is about changing your focus from trying to *do* anything and everything, to seeking Him and asking Him to change you. Truly this is about what *He* is going to do and surrendering to the recognition that we are unable to do anything to make this change happen."

"In addition," explained Sharon, "we must be willing to let our purpose in life be different". If Jen wanted to continue focusing on finding a husband and gaining her idealized life, there would be no change. Sharon stressed that Jen would need to be willing to shift her focus to God and becoming like Him.

This choice was hard for Jen. She did want what God wanted for her and was beginning to see she could not find peace without allowing Him to change her. At the same time, she was not ready to let go of her dreams. *Why couldn't that also be part of the plan for her?* The wrestling continued.

Discussion Questions

1. Take a few minutes to read the Sermon on the Mount in Matthew chapters 5 through 7. In light of what you have read here, how do you interpret these passages now?

2. As you think of righteousness happening from the inside out, how does this affect your understanding of the Sermon on the Mount?

3. How have you been trying to live out the law and all of Scripture? When have you tried to do it relying on God's strength? What difference have you noticed?

4. What have some of your motives been for serving God and for where you put your priorities? Where is your focus: on God and collaborating with Him, or more on yourself? How so?

11

When Branches Flourish

The journey has been challenging thus far. I am glad you're still with me. We have nearly crossed the valley floor and the rise will be coming soon. Before we start up, we have one more important perspective from Jesus' teachings to examine. Jesus has a master plan that He, the Father, and the Spirit came up with so that we could attain abundant life and connection with Him. Jesus said,

> I am the true vine, and my Father is the gardener. He cuts off every branch in me that bears no fruit, while every branch that does bear fruit he prunes so that it will be even more fruitful. You are already clean because of the word I have spoken to you. Remain in me, as I also remain in you. No branch can bear fruit by itself; it must remain in the vine. Neither can you bear fruit unless you remain in me. I am the vine; you are the branches. If you remain in me and I in you, you will bear much fruit; apart from me you can do nothing. (John 15:1–5)

In this metaphor, Jesus describes an interplay between us and God in His three distinct persons and teaches about dependence on Him, even as He demonstrates the submission that exists within the Godhead. Jesus is revealing that when we accept His salvation, we become a part of a deeply intertwined relationship with Him. Jesus is the vine we are connected to as branches. He is our connection because of what He has done for us.

Jesus is also the source who allows the Holy Spirit to be given to us. The Spirit submits to Jesus. In John 16:14, Jesus says, "He will glorify me because it is from me that he will receive what he will make known to you." The Spirit is the power that flows through us to create the fruit that He desires in us.

The Father is the gardener who tends to everything. Jesus submits to Him. This submission within the Godhead is done by choice. In John 5:19 Jesus said, "Very truly I tell you, the Son can do nothing by himself; he can do only what he sees his Father doing, because whatever the Father does the Son also does" and then again in verse 30, He says, "By myself I can do nothing; I judge only as I hear, and my judgment is just, for I seek not to please myself but him who sent me."

While, like Paul before his conversion, we can do many things without depending on Jesus, the things that matter—that will go with us into eternity—require a different focus. Many of us desire to live a life that has *real* value and impact, and Jesus demonstrates that the only way to have this God-given desire met is to rely on Him.

This eternal value plays out in the bearing of spiritual fruit. Paul says in Galatians 5:22–23, "But, the fruit of the Spirit is love, joy, peace, forbearance [patience], kindness, goodness, faithfulness, gentleness and self-control." These are the characteristics Jesus speaks of as well.

Notice though, these are the fruit of *the Spirit*, not the fruit of *our efforts*. They come from Him. We cannot make these things become our character by force of will. Certainly, we can behave more lovingly and with more patience and self-control, but for real deep character change to occur, the Holy Spirit must be at work in us. For us to be able to love our enemies, for instance, there must be a spiritual change from within.

I say this as an encouragement. We do not have to feel guilty or get down on ourselves when we are not doing well in these areas. Instead, we can recognize our weaknesses as humans, without guilt, and surrender them to God. We can ask *Him* to develop all of these things in our lives.

Oftentimes He develops these characteristics in us through trials. For whatever reason, that is the best and most effective means for us to change as humans. Remember, He is God. He knows us completely and He has far greater perspective and wisdom than we ever could. We do not even have the wisdom and clarity of thought to fully understand *ourselves* as well as He does. Instead of resisting, lean into the trials and allow the changes to come from Him.

Some of you may not see getting more education as a trial, but God sent me back to school to get my master's degree as a means to refine me. Most people who know me now find it hard to believe that was difficult for me. However, school has always been a challenge. So when I felt Him prompting me to return to school full-time without a clear direction of what the career on the other side would be, it was a real step of faith for me. He was gentle with me though.

You see, I had taken a couple of courses in order to understand my Bible better and ended up taking a course that involved touring the Bible lands of Israel. During this amazing trip, I met someone who inspired me to want to follow God more closely. Though it was not clear what God was going to ask, a niggling began within me that something important was coming. Then, one night when my father was in town we went out for dinner and I told him about my trip and the young man I had met. We talked in the parking lot of his hotel long after we arrived to drop him off. I remember crying as I realized I thought God was asking me to quit my job and go back to school full-time. That was a big ask!

God did not make it clear what He wanted me to do after I finished. I had been enrolled in the Religious Studies program so I could understand Scripture better, but I had not intended to complete the program. I certainly had no intention of changing careers. But during that conversation, the conviction was so strong, I could not ignore it.

My mother was shocked that I wanted to leave my stable career to return to school. She was concerned about what I might do afterward. Reflecting on it now, I wonder if she may have been concerned because she also knew well that I had never been a strong student. Community college was one thing; this was university.

Even so, I was determined to follow God's leading. This prompting remained strong for the almost six months before I had to enroll. I kept praying for Him to show me if I was not hearing correctly. When the time came, I obeyed, though I did so with fear and trembling.

During that first year I took a New Testament course, along with biblical interpretation, theology, and the other required courses. I came to understand God and His word much more than I had ever expected. Studying remained a challenge, but the difference was that this time I relied on God and was determined to see it through. I would pray regularly when I went to read or study. I knew I could not do this kind of study without His help.

I also learned about surrender and following Jesus in such a way that I could really become a disciple. I recall learning about the Sabbath rest and felt again that God was calling me to risk and rely on Him more. For me to study and yet not burn out, I needed a day of rest.

I read very slowly, so a day of not studying was a scary proposition. Once again, I decided I would risk obedience. *Somehow*, after I took one full day off per week, I was able to get all of my reading completed in less time and with better comprehension.

After my first complete year at the university, one of my professors encouraged me to enroll in the seminary instead. My marks ended up being very high in his course and others (another baffling thing for me and evidence of God's hand in this journey).

Although my college diploma would not count as a university degree in the requirements for the seminary, he believed so strongly in me that he talked to the dean and assisted in my being accepted as a mature student.

That had never happened to me before. In addition, this was an even bigger step of faith for me. *How could I, someone who hates school, be going to seminary to receive a master's degree?* To be honest, I still think that was crazy when I think about "the me" before He took control. Again, I obeyed God's leading and entered the seminary to work toward a Masters of Divinity with a counseling major.

Through this journey, God continued to ask me to do more than I could do in my own strength, and He continued to come through. Before you think it was all easy, I will admit, sometimes His coming through did not turn out as I expected, and sometimes it was quite painful.

In this situation, I was the branch. I did not create the fruit; I did not prune myself. I clung to the vine and He led me and nourished me so I could grow. He kept me safely connected. I was freed by not having to figure everything out. You, too, can use the metaphor of being a branch to find freedom. We are not supposed to be the vine, the gardener, or the one creating fruit. We are spiritually lifeless until we are grafted into the vine.

This is not "worm theology," which says we are nothing and have no value. The reality is that branches need the nutrients the main vine provides to survive and thrive. Branches are needed to produce the fruit. God created us for this purpose. It is an honored role, in fact.

Our role, therefore, is to stay connected to the vine and allow the gardener to prune anything that prevents us from producing the fruit. In those early years, He began the extensive work of pruning self-sufficiency from me; I imagine that for most of us self-dependence will continue to need pruning. That pruning allowed patience, joy, and faithfulness to grow in me, a process that continues today.

At the same time, we are not to keep checking out how we are changing, but to focus on Jesus Himself. As we get to know Him more and allow Him to make changes, the fruit will grow naturally. I love it when clients begin to experience this and report how well they responded in a situation where they usually responded poorly. It is exciting when we can "watch" ourselves have more patience or peace in situations that would normally derail us.

The focus on Jesus enables us to live out the standards that we see in the Bible, as intended. Jesus is consistent in teaching that what is most important in life—how to please God—is knowing Him and allowing Him to change us from the inside out.

God taught this in the Old Testament as well. Throughout the psalms and the prophets, the writers declare that God does not want sacrifices and offerings; He wants a change of heart. Even though He established the sacrificial law, His main interest was not in the sacrifices themselves. Through Hosea in 6:6 (NLT) God declares, "I want you to show love, not offer sacrifices. I want you to know me more than I want burnt offerings." He was not interested in His people just keeping the letter of the law, but in their attitudes as they did so.

In *Conformed to His Image*, Kenneth Boa contrasts the two extremes of legalism and license and concludes that God is actually calling us to live in liberty. Legalism is about trying to do everything by our own strength to become humanly righteous. License is about focusing only on God's grace and missing His calling to be holy. Jesus did not save us so we could simply pursue our own happiness and pleasure. Both of these extremes miss the point and purpose of God's work in our lives.

Liberty is about finding profound freedom in relying on God to transform our thinking and inclinations so that we can live as He requires. This is about an internal change that results in

> What is most important in life… is knowing Him and allowing Him to change us from the inside out.

behavioral change. So, as branches, we cling to the vine and the gardener prunes us to make way for a greater yield of fruit.

The gardener uses life circumstances to prune us and grow us for our own good. These can include doing small things like allowing daily irritants to continue in order to cut out selfishness and, instead, seek Him for more patience and perspective. They can be bigger things like the loss of a job to turn us from dependence on ourselves to Him.

This pruning often comes in the form of conviction (not guilt) for things we need to let go of or change. He will bring attitudes, thoughts, and behaviors to our attention that are not in accordance with the holiness He is creating in us. The focus is never on us *being* bad or wrong; it is on what needs to change. God is gentle in His convictions but also clear and unwavering.

At times the pruning can be quite drastic. For example, when my husband is working in our yard he uses tools ranging from small clippers to large pruners to deadhead and shape shrubs and trees. Sometimes he removes healthy branches because they are competing with another branch, increasing the risk of disease or a smaller yield. God also works this way. If our focus on good things is crowding out our focus on Him or our effectiveness in things that He has for us, He will prune them.

Striving and perfectionism are things that God will often cut out. Most of our churches need more volunteers. For those who are already active, this creates pressure to do more. Unfortunately, when we spread ourselves too thin we are no longer as effective in the areas where God wants us to serve. At times, He will allow us to burn out to deal with this striving. Through the painful recovery, we must learn how to say no, how to recognize what is for us and what is not for us to do. We also learn to rely on Him more rather than on our own strength.

God is the one who brings to completion the good work *He* began in us—we do not (Phil 1:6). Over time, you may get tired of being pruned and want to resist or disobey. Many of us have often cried out, half in jest, that we have enough "character". Others are simply tired and want the process to stop because it is tiring and painful.

Writing this brought to mind a new resistance band I am using for my work out because the last one no longer challenged me. This new one challenges me too much. I could go back to the other one, but that would not help me build muscle and tone. I have to experience muscle fatigue to achieve the results I am looking for. God's pruning is painful and tiring, but for us to achieve the results He wants, we must experience "character development fatigue."

Recall that we are connected to Him and that He will take care of us. Like a young child who in a moment of danger runs to his mother for protection and comfort, we can return to God. During storms, we can remind ourselves that the roots of mature vines go deep and thus we can be assured that we will not be lost. The vine holds firm as we hold firm to Him.

As we continue to work with the Holy Spirit, we find that things that were hard to avoid no longer interest us. We have patience with an older person; we have compassion for people who struggle with things we don't understand. In the midst of a rush, we can take the extra minute to be kind to a person who wants our attention; we can take time to play with our children instead of moving on to the next thing on our never-ending to do list. We want to give to those in need now rather than wait until we have "extra."

We also have a strong built-in warning system. We sense when temptations may be too strong and know what is needed to avoid them. We become attuned to the motives of others and are able to lovingly set boundaries with those who would seek to take advantage of us. The changes will occur naturally, and without pressure or striving; sometimes we suddenly realize that we are responding differently.

As the weeks moved further away from her mother's passing, Amanda and her dad struggled to figure out how to move forward without her. The carefree life Amanda had known had abruptly ended, and she fought to find her balance.

Initially, she had been angry at God, but that shifted to recognizing her need for Him. Her dad had taken the death very hard, and his way of coping was to throw himself into work. This left Amanda to fend for herself most of the time.

In those times she cried out to God with a new desperation. Slowly, Amanda came to the realization that this was the time to make her faith her own. She knew she needed renewed security, and God was the only one who could really understand. Friends meant well, but none of them had ever had a parent die.

When she spoke with one of her pastors, they talked about her grief and how she was going to move forward. He listened to her and empathized. He also encouraged her to continue seeking out God and His comfort, trusting that He is still good and loves her very much.

She shared her guilt over not spending more time with her mother. Again, the pastor was empathetic and assured her that her mother knew her love and God would readily forgive this.

In seeking God more, Amanda wrestled with her past sin and her continued desire to return to it—after all, it had usually felt so good. She knew this line of thinking was not helpful, and she really wanted to make both God and her mom proud. At the same time, she knew her own heart was not in line with her mind. So, remembering the advice her mother had often provided in times of struggle, Amanda begged God to change her.

To her surprise, instead of God simply taking the desire away, one of her old boyfriends, Jared, connected with her on social media to offer condolences. He also suggested they get together and "reconnect" for old-time sake.

He had been a nice enough guy, but their relationship had gone way too far on so many levels. She knew she could easily fall back into intimacy with him and cried out to God asking, "why are you doing this when I am trying to do things better?"

Immediately, the thought occurred that God might have brought Jared back in answer to her prayer. *Would God work that way?* Before she responded to Jared though, she spent time in prayer surrendering her weakness and temptation and asking God for wisdom on how to respond. He knew how lonely she was and how great it would feel to be comforted, she realized. She also realized He was not judging her for that. She felt safe with God, even talking to Him about this sinful desire.

As she continued to ask God for help, she began to feel a new resolve. She knew seeing Jared would not help her and would only make her feel worse. With tentative strength, she wrote an email, thanking Jared for his kind words of sympathy, but turning him down on reconnecting personally. As she pressed the send button, her strength increased. She knew she had done the right thing. She also knew God was changing her, one baby step at a time.

She thanked Him, knowing many more of these "opportunities" would likely come, but feeling more hopeful that real change—internal change—was possible. This time she accepted her own weakness without shame and did not try to change it in her own strength. She had relied on God, and in a very small and quiet way He had given what was needed.

Perhaps this is what it means when the Bible says, "when you are tempted, [God] will also provide a way out so that you can endure it" (1 Cor 10:13). He had made a way out of an appealing situation when she was willing to listen. She realized that she was finally accepting that she needed His way out instead of her own. It somehow felt comforting and liberating.

Now that your eyes have adjusted a bit, can you see the light filtering through? Only a little further now and we start our ascent.
Let's keep going!

Discussion Questions

1. When you think of your role as a branch, how does this affect how you see your relationship with and responsibility to God? Do you feel fear or trepidation at the thought of letting go of control of the outcomes in your life? How do you feel knowing that when you cooperate with God, the results of your life are no longer up to you?

2. How is God asking or prompting you to step out in faith? Or how has He? If He is, what holds you back? What in this chapter has encouraged you to let go and die to self a little more in order to enjoy what God has for you?

Part III

Dying to Self Changes Everything

We are at the border of truth about ourselves. Here, we pause and turn our view inward. You see, this surrendering to God must be about more than simply what we do and how we relate to Him and the world. It is also about how we see and relate to ourselves in light of what He has done for us. An understanding of who God says we are frees us from the constraints of our mistaken beliefs that inhibit and misguide us. Surveying our inner terrain may be terrifying but it is the most liberating aspect of our journey.

We will explore our identities, our purpose, and what it really means to die to self in a personal way. Through this process, we will come to more fully appreciate the richness and beauty that can be found in fully surrendering to God and allowing Him to lead and control our lives, no matter how they end up.

12

Understanding our Inherited Identities

On this inward part of our journey, we'll first look at our identity—who we really are—because an accurate identity paradoxically frees us from focusing too much on ourselves and allows us to naturally focus on God and others. Often we have a disconnect between how God sees us and what He wants for us and how we have come to see ourselves and our potential. Sometimes the disconnect is even between who we think we are and the characteristics and thoughts we actually exhibit.

If you have been a Christian for a while, you may know cognitively that you are a child of God, which means you are accepted, secure, and significant, but you may not understand what that means in reality. Many of us may not deeply believe it because we have also been shaped inwardly by false messages that affect our behavior. This is a result of living in a fallen world.

Possibly starting when we were very young, others have spoken messages over us that shaped our identity, or we intuitively picked up beliefs based on how people treated us or how situations seemed to always play out. How we have come to see ourselves is the filter through which we interpret all experiences going forward. An interior survey helps us recognize what parts of our identity we need to bring into submission to God.

Generally, we tend to have one of four overarching identity styles, depending on the relational experiences we've had with close family members and caregivers growing up. However, these identities play out differently in each of us. These identities are commonly called: anxious/preoccupied, avoidant, disorganized, and secure, though these labels do not necessarily resonate with our experiences. For instance, disorganized has nothing to do with organizational skills. We will use them here for classification purposes, but let's not get too caught up in the possible definitions of the labels themselves.

Those of us who have the first overarching identity, anxious/preoccupied, have come to believe we are not worthy, not loveable, and/or not valuable in and of ourselves. Or perhaps we believe we are not smart or not capable enough in some or many ways. In general, we believe we do not measure up to others.

Worry and doubt may have plagued us at different points of our life and anxiety may be a common companion. Perhaps we regularly seek the wisdom and guidance of others, believing they know better and can make better decisions than we can. We tend to aim to please and long to be accepted by others and so, unfortunately, we may find that people seem to take advantage of us. Assertiveness is a challenge because we fear disappointing others and we are not confident in our abilities or personal value.

When it comes to God, while we may know in our head that He loves us, we really question why. We believe all that the Scriptures say about one's worth once we belong to God, but somehow cannot accept that we really have value. We see clearly the worth others have; yet, it simply doesn't make sense for us in light of our experiences.

For a long time, this was me. During my high school years and early twenties, I really didn't like myself very much and sought the approval of others to give me value. When that didn't happen, or didn't happen the way I'd hoped, I internalized it as a reflection of my lack of worth. It wasn't until I was working on my master's degree that this started to change.

During that time my relationship with God continued to deepen. My counseling courses encouraged me to look deeper within myself and understand who I was and what has contributed to how I see myself. In my Spiritual Direction courses I gained greater understanding of surrender and allowing God to define me instead of allowing others, or even what I believed about myself at the time, to define me. Even so, my increase in security and confidence were very slow. Even now these old belief systems can trip me up. However, I am able to identify them now and bring them back in line with the truth I choose to depend on. But, I'm getting ahead of myself.

If we are in the second overarching group, avoidant, we know we are capable, and, in fact, believe we are the only one who can take care of "me". We believe that everyone else has, and most likely will, let us down, and so it is up to us to make our own way. While on some level, we may think it would be nice to let others in, allowing them to see our pain or needs and assist us, we are very uncomfortable with taking that kind of risk. Overall, we view needing others, or anything from them, for that matter, as weak. When we do wonder what it would be like to let someone in, we remind ourselves of the times when we have tried and it did not work. We reason that the risk of vulnerability is just too great. It is safer and more comfortable to stay protected within our self-sufficiency.

Some of us are not even aware of our needs and do not allow ourselves to really feel emotional pain or distress. We also learned early on that our feelings and pain are not important and we should ignore or control them. We may believe most emotions are weak and get in the way.

For this group, God is there, and we may sincerely want to know and please Him. At the same time, the idea of actually *relying* on Him in day-to-day life seems, well, unnecessary. The concept of intimacy with Him also seems strange and intangible. We know we need Him for salvation, and we are quite aware of our sins that only He can atone for. We readily admit we need

Him for that. However, it is difficult to imagine giving Him full control. *What does that even mean, anyway?*

We may have bought into the belief that "God helps those who help themselves." In fact, many people believe this is a verse from Scripture, but it isn't. That belief comes from our driven culture rather than from God. Frankly, for us, helping ourselves is more empowering as a way of living. After all, we have proven we are capable.

If we are in the third group, disorganized, we live in a very uncertain world where we often do not like ourselves and cannot trust ourselves to do anything well. At the same time, we view others as being unsafe because so many people have hurt us deeply throughout our lives. At times, we believe we are alone and need to depend on ourselves; at other times that feels like too much and we reach out, only to be hurt or betrayed again. Things never seem to work out and we blame ourselves for it. We think there must be something fundamentally wrong with us for life to be this way.

When it comes to God, we are thankful for His acceptance and forgiveness, and yet we fear whether we can trust that part of Him. We believe we have a fundamental flaw and so we wait for God to be punitive. We believe we deserve punishment and that we cannot have the full experience of grace that others receive. We want to believe, but the risk is too great. It is better to expect the worst. That way, we reason, we will not be as hurt when it inevitably comes.

Many of us do not, however, fall into any of these groups. We feel fairly secure and know we have value, though sometimes we doubt ourselves, like anyone can. We also feel it is fairly safe to trust and rely on others, and are able to discern who is likely to be trustworthy and who is not. Though there have been challenges in life, we can feel fairly confident about navigating them and, for the most part, have fared okay.

Even so, we have areas in our life we know are not surrendered to God, and we have doubt, insecurity, or worry about those places. Within our relationship with Him, we may be at different levels of dependence versus self-sufficiency, in various areas. We may also be torn between wanting to go deeper or not go deeper.

Regardless of our identity style, many people believe that how we behave determines who we are. In reality, who we *believe* ourselves to be determines how we behave. Some of us pretend, even to ourselves, that we believe one thing, but ultimately, we will act out of the beliefs we truly hold. The good news is that, in cooperation with God, we can change our beliefs about ourselves and thus our behaviors. While real change in belief takes intentionality, repetition, and time, it is possible.

One barrier to change can be our lack of awareness about our belief systems. Many are easy to recognize in the way we talk to ourselves, but not everyone has learned to observe and recognize their self-talk. Other beliefs are hidden from our conscious thoughts and function more as underlying "facts" that do not need to be articulated. We simply act and react without being aware of the regulating force behind our behavior.

For instance, we may not realize we believe that others cannot be trusted, but when we interact with others we would tend to be more reserved about sharing personal details or being vulnerable. Others, whose underlying belief is that vulnerability is a weakness, do not hold this conviction because they think people are not trustworthy. Rather, they believe they should never let others see their vulnerability and put themselves in a position of weakness. So, the behavior may be similar but the underlying beliefs can be different.

Sometimes, though, we can figure out what we may believe by thinking and praying about how we are behaving. If we do not explore and articulate these beliefs, however, we will continue our behaviors.

> In reality, who we *believe* ourselves to be determines how we behave.

The hope in all of this is that, regardless of our histories and how we have lived, our beliefs and perspectives can change. Our minds can be renewed. We have learned from neuroscience that with enough focus and intentional thought our brains can literally be rewired. We can become aware of our belief systems by exploring them as we go through different experiences. Through this process we can then evaluate our convictions and decide if these beliefs are working for us. If they aren't, we can slowly work at considering and adopting alternative interpretations and beliefs about ourselves and life experiences.

Through this intentional process, new neurological connections are made and strengthened. As a result, our beliefs change, and we start feeling and acting differently. Again, this takes effort and time, but it is possible.

During this exploration, our goal is not to judge ourselves or our behaviors; rather, it is to make an *open and curious* consideration of patterns and how these came to be. We can then begin to gently challenge those belief systems with truth and experiment with new perspectives to see if our experiences change in light of new alternative potential beliefs.

Think of it this way, if a miracle happened tonight and you woke up the person you always wished you could be, what would be different about how you interacted with yourself and others? Consider concrete things that might be different and then behave as though those things were true. Does this change the way you interact or how others interact with you? In this way, you are "trying on" new perspectives to see how they impact your life.

Some people can make these shifts themselves. For them, it's a matter of being open to seeing a different perspective, regardless of how life has played out thus far. Even if we do not have a balanced sense of security with self and/or others, this can be learned. It is not easy, but with intentional effort, perspectives can change and thus, how we experience life can change—radically.

Others may need outside counsel to gain insights into themselves and to learn how to move ahead. There is no shame in that, just as there is none in going to a specialist for weight loss. When belief systems are ingrained, often we need the perspective of someone else to see the alternatives that seem hidden from us. Our internal critics can be relentless in holding us to negative belief systems and it is difficult to counter these alone.

Even when we have severe mental or emotional disorders, we can learn to relate differently to ourselves and thus change the influence of the disorder. Here, I am talking about how we *experience* life. Our identity is not connected to our experience in a cause-effect fashion. Instead, our experiences and our interpretations of them develop out of what we understand our identity to be.

Naturally, in our early years we come to understand ourselves based on our experiences. Yet often our early experiences do not speak accurately into our identities. We can hold mistaken beliefs from that time because our brains were not developed enough to have perspective or fully comprehend all that was going on.

For instance, when someone grows up in a home with parents who often fight, it is natural for that child to believe that it is their fault that their parents clashed. Children's brains have not developed to the point that they can separate themselves from the events around them. They truly believe they are the cause of, or have significant influence on, the events even when they have nothing to do with them.

An example of someone who strongly believes something that is not true would be a person with severe anorexia. Those on the outside see the person emaciated and long to make them see what they are doing to themselves. The person with anorexia has a distorted view of being an unacceptably overweight person. They cannot see at all what others see.

Even our biggest mistakes cannot define us permanently. Similarly, great sin done against us, such as abuse, does not have to continue to scar us, to keep us in shame, because we can come to see ourselves differently. Our past does not *define* us. It makes an impact and influences who we are, but we do not have to let it mark us forever. While the past remains, we can move beyond it to a far better, free way of living. We can trust God for change because beliefs simply do not have power to hold us if we don't want them to. This is where the hope comes from. Our beliefs don't actually *make* things true.

Unfortunately, most people do not realize change is possible or if they do, they avoid making the effort. On the one hand, some argue that their pain or history isn't really so bad and convince themselves they don't need to work with God on a healthier identity. Alternatively, others become frustrated with the notion of change because they feel it invalidates just how bad things are or were. They may not be ready to let go of feeling the pain or of justifying their behaviors.

Please know, I appreciate how hard this struggle can be—excruciatingly so, at times. Please also know that we are coming up against a powerful belief system. But be assured that anything that has shaped our *interpretation* of self and life did not shape our *actual* identity. Our actual identity comes from God, who says we are highly valued, accepted, loved, and complete. He knows better than we do. That assurance can change how we see all experiences—no matter how great or how small—that helped develop us. Bear with me in this. We'll get there.

As Linda continued to wrestle with her mother's confession and story of transformation, she realized she wanted change in her own life. She had always been a hard-slugging person, but she wanted more peace, too. *Maybe life did not have to be this hard all the time*, she pondered. She was not ready to reconsider God in this, though. She wanted to look at other options.

This began a journey of self-exploration. She purchased self-help books that had her looking into her history and belief systems. As she diligently worked through them, she came to recognize that she really did not trust people or the world in general. She truly believed she could only fully rely on herself. This wasn't really a shock, but the idea that she might be attracting people or situations that tended to perpetuate this belief system surprised her.

She contemplated whether her continued reserve and stand-offishness had really pushed people away from being sensitive to her. *In her striving to succeed and show the world that she didn't need anyone, could she have bulldozed over people and invited resistance from others?* She knew she had been hard on other people, *but at the time they seemed so problematic,* and now she wondered if people had never really warmed to her because she wasn't willing to let them see her vulnerable side.

This perspective jarred Linda. Being vulnerable had never sat well with her and she had learned to shun vulnerability and openness in childhood. And yet, she respected people who were able to be vulnerable. They didn't seem weak. *Even so, there had to be another way.*

She also began to see how she may have contributed to some of her relational break-downs. Her first husband was abusive, but as she thought back, she could admit that she was abusive to him as well in her attempts to protect herself.

Trying to lighten her thoughts, she joked with herself that she must be getting old to be reflecting so much. And yet, she knew it wasn't age, it was her longing for the peace she saw in her mom.

Linda and John both found some aspects of his changes as a Christian difficult. He often asked for more connection and intimacy. Sex was never the problem, but he wanted her to be more open with him, to let him understand her feelings, fears, and motivations. *"This vulnerability thing keeps coming up!"* she lamented to herself. And, that kind of intimacy terrified Linda.

However, over the months since John's conversion, he had been pulling away from her sexually, saying he really didn't think they should be having sex since they were not married. He said he still wanted her, but was beginning to want what God wanted more.

Everything about that felt very unsafe for Linda. John had brought up the idea of marriage, but both were cautious now, particularly with her resistance to his new faith. They both knew what the Bible said about not marrying someone of a different faith system. Further, his shift in allegiance to God added to her feeling unsafe.

She wrestled with being willing to be more vulnerable. She didn't want to push John away, but she couldn't trust that he would truly accept her being estranged from God. She was certain God wanted nothing to do with her, and thought that, as John got closer to Him, perhaps he wouldn't want her either. Even so, she knew she had to keep looking at herself, if she wanted to find peace. This was not really about John; it was about her.

Discussion Questions

1. Take a few minutes to think about how you see yourself. What are some of your positive, affirming beliefs? What negative beliefs come up? How long have you believed these things?

2. Which identity group do you most resonate with? Do you feel mostly insecure and in need of others to validate you? Or do your fears relate more to others not being able to meet your needs, thus leaving you to do it on your own? Do you tend to waver between these two, feeling like you need the validation, yet not really believing anyone is actually capable of doing that for you? Or, do you tend to feel fairly secure and able to have healthy, open relationships, but you know there are areas where you are not surrendered to God and find that a challenge? How does this affect how you see your relationship with God?

13

Understanding our Expectations

Now that we have a better understanding of our perceived identities, let's look deeper into how they can affect our relationship with ourselves, others, and God. They have an impact because how we act and react is determined by what we believe about ourselves.

If we have a healthy identity, we are able to separate ourselves from the responses of others and remain secure. In doing so, we are able to remain consistent and behave out of our positive belief systems, rather than bouncing off others or reacting in unhealthy ways. However, if we have negative expectations because of what we learned growing up, we can often invite negative responses. Alternatively, some of us hold unrealistic positive expectations in our effort to counter what we have absorbed. Both types of expectations may lead to frustration and, as a result, our perceived identity may be damaged. This is simply a natural outcome of our belief systems.

Let's consider some examples to make the pattern clearer. If we believe that others are better than us and will reject us, we may approach situations feeling anxious and unsure. To protect ourselves, we may focus on what we are doing or saying in an effort to make sure we don't look stupid. As a result, instead of presenting our real, loveable self to the others, we appear to be aloof or closed off.

In conversation, we may not be able to focus on the other person because we are listening to our own self-talk. We are likely beating ourselves up over what we have said or over the other person's reaction to us. The other person, who is not aware of this internal struggle, only picks up signals indicating we are not interested in what they are saying. As a result, they end the conversation quickly and look for someone else who seems more interested in them. In turn, we feel rejected—yet again—and our expectations are realized.

Yet, even if we fear rejection, we can have a much better outcome when we remind ourselves of who we really are—acceptable, intelligent, capable, and so on—and intentionally focus on the other person. The anxiety may still be there, but because we are not focused on it, others are not aware of what is going on inside us. Rather they feel heard and sense that we are interested in them and are more likely to continue the conversation.

Another example is how the fear of saying "no" can lead to being regularly taken advantage of. Naturally, we do not like this, and yet our fear of rejection or judgment if we say "no" or if we set boundaries, keeps us stuck. People will think they know what is okay or not for us, because we seem to be fine with how they treat us. After all, we are kind and appear eager to please. In turn, we feel taken advantage of and not valued. Yet, we just can't let others know what our real boundaries are and what is too much.

However, when we know that our value and worth are not related to what we do or what others think of us, we will find it easier to set clear boundaries. We will be able to clearly and politely let others know our limits. Paradoxically, others will respect this and will abide, or learn to abide, by our boundaries. When others know what we define as being acceptable, it makes it easier to get along, and generally we will feel respected and valued.

Alternatively, expecting too much of others because we feel we are not skilled, attractive, or smart enough, for example, can lead to a self-fulfilling prophecy of others pushing us away and rejecting us. When others do not come through the way we would like them to, we feel hurt. When people say "no," we feel rejected.

This pain of rejection and not knowing our self-worth may be so strong that we tend to seek more from others in an effort to ward off these feelings. Unfortunately, when others do not feel that their "no" is respected, they may push us further away, which confirms our beliefs that we are too much for others to take, even while we feel as though we are not valuable or worthy.

If this describes you, coming to know your true value and identity will allow you to realize that even when others are not able to meet your needs, you are okay. You'll feel accepted by God, knowing that He sees and understands your needs and can provide for you. This does not mean He *will* always give you exactly what you want, but that He will comfort you and support you in any disappointment. He can free you from letting your identity, value, or worth be determined by His response to your perceived needs. We can be okay, regardless of our circumstances, when we truly know who God is and who we are in Him.

The highly driven person who is compelled to achieve may feel shaken if they are no longer able to succeed in new areas or even to keep going in their current ones. If you tend to be driven, knowing your value apart from what you do will allow you to have more peace. You will no longer depend on achievement or be broken by a failure; you'll rest in the truth that you are still valued and significant.

Even when we have a fairly secure understanding of self, we can be thrown by unanticipated changes if we rely on life experience to confirm our identity. Sometimes life simply does not work out as we expect, and if our trust is in life consistently meeting our expectations, our perceived identity can be shaken.

For instance, being downsized can challenge the internal stability of someone whose identity is connected to performance. This is particularly true if the person cannot find another job as quickly as they anticipated.

A dear friend has gone through many such work-life problems. A business he started was immobilized by the recession and then a partner he took on to keep it afloat tarnished his reputation with less than honorable business practices. My friend had to step away from the business. When he did get other work, he led a series of successful projects that were taken from him just before he could receive credit for his efforts. Many times, he felt like he was being put out to pasture while another profited by his efforts.

I imagine that he was tempted to take this personally, which would have brought him down. He, however, allowed these experiences to move him to dig into God and receive his value and worth from Him, rather than from the outcome of his hard work. Throughout the years, my friend has learned a deeper trust and dependence on God, which allows him to not be shaken or brought low when things don't turn out as he expected or even how they should have based on his good intentions and diligence.

Many Millennials find entering the work force challenging, and sometimes distressing, because they expect to readily find a good position. Many in this generation tend to believe that they can succeed and rise quickly in their careers based on who they are. They don't take into account the work they produce.

If they feel capable of performing at a certain level, the idea of having to start at the bottom and work up to the level they feel capable of working at upsets them; it feels beneath them. Their challenge is to accept that while their value *is* important in succeeding, being able to follow established procedures and fit within organizational culture is also necessary. Millennials with an identity based on God will not be as thrown because they know their position in an organization does not define their identity or worth. Their security is not rocked.

Whether we have problems with self-fulfilling negative prophecies or deeply internalized expectations that are not being met, the key to overcoming life's obstacles is understanding that our identity is not tied to anything external. Our identity can be secure and solid regardless of how life and relationships play out. Who we *are* remains intact when our foundation is built on the solid rock of God; we will be able to stand firm.

This is so important to God because it returns us to our intended identities in Him. In *My Utmost for His Highest*, Oswald Chambers reminds us that we were created to bring God glory and to enjoy Him. When we are bogged down by trying to find our identity in anything other than Him, we go against our created nature and thus go off our intended path. Things are more difficult for us off the path. God loved us so much that He sent His Son to die on a cross (John 3:16) so that we could be restored to our intended identities and purpose.

God once took me to the end of myself to show me that failure did not have to define me. During my master's studies, God started showing me that my real identity did not come from the approval of others. God kept working with me on dying to self and my shifting mistaken beliefs that a need to perform could replace my need for approval.

Early in my second year, I felt God prompting me to get a second major, this one in pastoral ministry. Now, I had no intention of being a pastor and I did not want to preach. The idea of speaking in front of others terrified me. *What could I possibly have to share?* As with other promptings from God, they did not lessen, but increased.

After about three or four months of wrestling and resisting, I arranged with the registrar to make the change. It would mean deferring my graduation another year, and therefore not graduating with my new friends. Even so, this is what He wanted, so I obeyed.

In order to get a major in pastoral ministry, I had to take four biblical language courses, with each one building on what had been learned in the previous course. I am *terrible* at learning languages. My brain simply does not make the connections. I went in fearfully but fully trusting that God would make my brain adapt. After all, He *had* enabled me to learn and read faster.

So, at the end of my second language course, when it was clear that I did not have the foundation and structure needed to continue with the third and fourth courses, my faith was rocked. I couldn't earn the second major. *Hadn't God been the one telling me to do this all along? He knew I wouldn't be able to do this! Why would He make me do this only to lead me to failure?* As I cried, wrestled, and grieved, I felt Him revealing that He is

> Even when I was at the end of myself, He seemed to assure me, "I AM."

still God. Even when I was at the end of myself, He seemed to assure me, "I AM."

I was still okay because of Him. Yes, He *had known* I would not be able to complete a second major. Yes, He had still directed me to add this program, with all of the sacrifices required. He was with me and I did not have to fear failure. The *results* of what He asked were not up to me. As long as I did my best (and I really did!), He would determine the outcome.

I still do not know why I had to get that minor (the second major was down-graded due to the incompletion of the remaining two language courses), other than to learn to face failure differently. I can honestly say I do not fear failure now. I don't like it—but I don't fear it. When I faced failure another time, I was able to get through it without letting it affect the security of my identity.

Do you remember James, who had a life changing illness that left him uncertain about everything? As he grappled with the bleak prognosis that his pain and fatigue would not likely go away, he realized that he no longer knew who he was.

His identity was so tied to his work, in being able to accomplish things and push forward, that he had no idea how to be himself without it. Even when he was considering retirement, he had intended to keep highly busy and involved. This disease had brought everything into question.

Naturally, his relationship with God was affected. At first he raged at God for allowing this to happen to him. He argued that he had always been a good Christian; he served when he could and he regularly tithed to the church. *With my income in the later years, that was a lot of money,* he argued. *How could You let this happen to one of Your faithful ones?*

Then he started to admit to himself that perhaps he hadn't been as faithful as he had claimed. He had put most of his energy into work rather than the church. *Was that why?* As he prayed, read the Bible, and wrestled, he came to see that life is not formulaic like that. Bad things happen simply because we live in a fallen state. Even so, James was again left with the desperate search to find out who he was now.

Anger at God would not bring relief. Instead, he needed to figure out a new identity for himself. He determined that he would not let this defeat him! *That* was not his character. Recognizing this renewed his hope. Even in all his pain, his determination remained. He could hold onto that. He was a conqueror. It occurred to him, *there is a Scripture that says that* (Romans 8:37). This got him back into the Word. *What else did it say about his identity?*

Discussion Questions

1. As you look at your behaviors in general and how you interact with others, what patterns do you think you could explore further (remember, explore with curiosity, not judgment)?

2. How do you think your beliefs about yourself affect how you interact with others? What would be different if you had different beliefs (keep this personal to who you actually are—the intent is not to pretend you are someone else)?

14 | Unmerited Identity

Scripture has a much higher view of our identity than we often do. At the same time, it has a realistic view because it roots our identity in God, who created and knows us better than we know ourselves, which means we can safely make that identity our own.

First of all, all people have high value simply because we are created in God's image. This means we are created with the capacity to reason, understand complexities, have abstract thought, create, relate to others, empathize, and intentionally make an impact on people and the world around us.

Beyond that, as believers who have accepted the free gift of salvation, we have so much more. Regardless of life circumstances, we can know and claim our identity in Christ; we can become the person He says we are. This is possible because, when we put our faith in Christ, we received the Holy Spirit and were adopted into God's family. The Apostle Paul said in Romans 8:14–17:

> For those who are led by the Spirit of God are the children of God. The Spirit you received does not make you slaves, so that you live in fear again; rather, the Spirit you received brought about your adoption to sonship. And by him we cry, *"Abba, Father."* The Spirit himself testifies with our spirit that we are God's children. Now if we are children, then we are heirs—heirs of God and co-heirs with Christ, if indeed we share in his sufferings in order that we may also share in his glory.

Did you catch the significance of our relationship with God? Not only has God adopted us as His own children, He has made us co-heirs with Christ Himself! We are sons and daughters of the Most High God, all rights and privileges included. This does mean, though, that we will also "share" in Jesus' suffering in this life, as well as in His glory. While suffering can diminish our old identities, it also makes room for our identity in Christ to grow and develop. We can claim and take courage in knowing we are fully accepted and secure as adopted children based on what He did and not on how our life plays out.

We are not foster children who are not legally secure with their foster families, and may be passed on at any time. We have been "legally" bound to God through adoption and we belong to Him. No one on earth, in the heavenly realms, or anywhere in all creation can remove us from His family (Jn 10:28–29; Rom 8:38–39). This also means that nothing we do or don't do can change this relationship. One thing we want to have clear: When we are saved and the Holy Spirit resides in us, He owns us. We do not own Him. We cannot kick Him out. More than that, when He lives within us, He changes us so that we do not want to remove Him. We are secure.

In *Victory over the Darkness,* Neil Anderson has a list of verses that speak of our acceptance, security, and significance in Christ. For this list, he turned biblical passages into I-statements. I have included them below for your reference.

Who I am In Christ

I am Accepted

John 1:12	I am God's child
John 15:15	I am Christ's friend
Romans 5:1	I have been justified

1 Corinthians 6:17	I am united with the Lord and one with Him in spirit
1 Corinthians 6:20	I have been bought with a price, I belong to God
1 Corinthians 12:27	I am a member of Christ's body
Ephesians 1:1	I am a saint
Ephesians 1:5	I have been adopted as God's child
Ephesians 2:18	I have direct access to God through the Holy Spirit
Colossians 1:14	I have been redeemed and forgiven of all my sins
Colossians 2:10	I am complete in Christ

I am Secure

Romans 8:1–2	I am free forever from condemnation
Romans 8:28	I am assured that all things work together for good
Romans 8:33–34	I am free from any condemning charges against me
Romans 8:35	I cannot be separated from the love of God
2 Corinthians 1:21	I have been established, anointed, and sealed by God
Colossians 3:3	I am hidden with Christ in God
Philippians 1:6	I am confident that the good work God has begun in me will be perfected

Philippians 3:20	I am a citizen of heaven
2 Timothy 1:7	I have not been given a spirit of fear but of power, love, and a sound mind
Hebrews 4:16	I can find grace and mercy in time of need
1 John 5:18	I am born of God and the evil one cannot touch me

I am Significant

Matthew 5:13–14	I am the salt and light of the earth
John 15:1, 5	I am a branch of the true vine, a channel of His life
John 15:16	I have been chosen and appointed to bear fruit
Acts 1:8	I am a personal witness of Christ's
1 Corinthians 3:16	I am God's temple
2 Corinthians 5:17–20	I am a minister of reconciliation
2 Corinthians 6:1	I am God's co-worker
Ephesians 2:6	I am seated with Christ in the heavenly realm
Ephesians 2:10	I am God's workmanship
Ephesians 3:12	I may approach God with freedom and confidence
Philippians 4:13	I can do all things through Christ who strengthens

All these affirmation statements are true of you, if you have received Christ as your savior. I have worked with many people who can accept these statements as truth in general but who really struggle with allowing them to define their identity. One exercise I often prescribe clients is to repeat one of these aloud each day, five times or more, placing their full name after the word "I." For instance, "I, Tara Lalonde, am God's child." Saying these affirmations sounds simple but many people really struggle with saying them aloud and including their names in them. The effort reveals areas where you may not deeply believe these truths about yourself. As you repeat them, they will slowly begin to sink in and you'll have new insights into the areas of resistance, enabling you to work on them.

In my first experience with an exercise like this I was instructed to say "I belong to God." It was during a spiritual direction course and we were working through *Space for God* by Don Postema. As I repeated this phrase, it took on different nuances as I emphasized different words. "*I, Tara Lalonde,* belong to God," "I, Tara Lalonde, *belong* to God," "I, Tara Lalonde, belong to *God.*" Can you hear the differences? I remember feeling deeply loved and accepted in a new way. Try that with your own name and allow Jesus to speak the nuances into your heart.

Another exercise I prescribe, and practice myself, is to regularly meditate on one of these truths throughout the day. Pick only one for the day or week and repeat it as it comes to mind and when you encounter challenges or difficulties. You can do this with any biblical truth or passage.

This exercise was especially helpful in one job I had. Once when my boss asked me to do something that frustrated me to no end, I walked down one of the halls to do his bidding repeating, "The Lord is my strength and my refuge," one of my favorite breath prayers (a prayer that can be said in one breath). By the time I reached my destination, my perspective had changed and I felt more in control. I will never forget that walk and the results of this simple exercise. I now regularly practice it when I need extra support from the Lord.

As you meditate (meditation is simply focused attention on a repeated word, phrase, or state) on the passages about your identity in Christ, they will reshape your belief systems about yourself. Then you will notice, through no effort of your own, that these truths are also changing how you relate and behave. Furthermore, you will come to naturally rely on your direct access to God as your ever-present resource in times of need (Psalm 46:1).

The changes continue. When we internalize that God values us, we no longer need to impress others or turn into pretzels to please them. Our acceptance and significance are secure. We can cease striving and rest in knowing that we are not required to do anything to gain our worth or value. God has already freely given it to us.

Paul says, "If God is for us, who can be against us?" (Rom 8:31). This does not mean that no one will ever oppose us; that certainly wasn't the case for him or his readers. Rather, it means that no one has the power to take away what God has given us. We will always have His unfathomable love. Even death is no threat to us, our identity in Him, or our place in His family. Our standing with Him is infinitely secure.

If this is your first time hearing these truths, they may sound a bit oversimplified. I get it. However, God promises that renewing your mind by focusing on what is true, noble, right, pure, lovely, admirable, excellent, and praiseworthy will change how you live and experience life (Rom 12:2; Phil 4:8). Often the process takes time, but the change will happen.

In both passages Paul is encouraging his audiences, including us, to change our thinking so as to align our beliefs with the truths God has given us. Paul says that in doing so, we will come to know God's perfect will and we will receive peace. While these passages do not directly refer to our identity, they do contain truths related to what we believe about ourselves and how we act and react.

If we are focused on negativity or believe we are less than what God says we are in light of what He has done for us, then we are not thinking on what is "right" or "true." As a result, our focus pulls us away from His truth and prevents us from living the life

He intended us to live, a life of freedom from lies and self-depre-cation, a life free from self-focus.

You see, once we internalize our identity as God sees it, we no lon-ger need to concentrate on it. We can then put our attention on Him and others because our own identity is entirely secure.

We can cease striving and rest in knowing that we are not required to do anything to gain our worth or value.

Further, the passage in Romans about transforming our minds *is* connected to how we see ourselves. In Romans 12:3, Paul instructs us to not "think of ourselves more highly than [we] ought," but to have "sober judgment" according to the faith God has given us. While many of us think this means that we should not be proud, this verse also means we should also not think of ourselves as lower than we are. Sober judgment works both ways. Unfortunately, many Christians believe that we should put our-selves down or belittle the value or talents that God has given us in order to be humble.

In *The Screwtape Letters*, C.S. Lewis depicts a senior demon instructing a junior demon on how to keep a man away from God and then, when the man becomes a Christian, on how to keep him from fully experiencing God. In one letter, the senior demon instructs his apprentice to try to convince the man that his skills or talents are less valuable than they are as a means of attaining humility. I love the way he describes God's real intent of humility. He writes,

> The Enemy [God] wants to bring the man to a state of mind in which he could design the best cathedral in the world, and know it to be the best, and rejoice in the fact, without being any more (or less) or otherwise glad at having done it than he would be if it had been done by another. The Enemy wants him, in the end, to be so free from any bias in his own favor that he can rejoice in his own talents as frankly and gratefully as in his neighbor's talents.

Keep in mind, that while we *are* highly valued by Him, we are not more highly valued than others. We are co-heirs together. This means that though we are at different points in our journeys with God, and thus are not healed of all the same things, we all share the same value and worth as children of God. We are in no position to look down upon others or judge them simply because of the things they do or struggle with that are not the things we do or struggle with.

Further, we are different and that is celebrated. In the novel, *The Shack*, William Young depicts God in human forms to help us understand God's nature. In one scene he has Papa (God the Father) saying that He is particularly fond of someone. He then explains that He is particularly fond of us all. I believe God does feel this way and celebrates the uniqueness He has created in all of us. He does not require us to be perfect in order to have value and be used by Him. We, too, can look at others as God's children and remember that He loves them as much as He loves us. God is working in them and extending grace to them even as He does for us. We don't need to compare ourselves.

Knowing that we have our value and identity from God and what He has done for us, gives us perspective on ourselves. Instead of needing to perform, we rest in humility and marvel at what God has done for us. This realization of our true identity naturally prompts us to live more like Christ. Because God empowers and equips us to do what He requires, we do not have to struggle on our own to develop Christ-like character. This is an ongoing process in which we partner with Him as He refines us. In the areas that do not come naturally, ask Him to equip you as He sees fit.

As we let go of the old core identities, and receive and surrender to the identities God is giving us, our actions naturally change. Because of this new belief system, we see the world differently. The things that used to hold power no longer do so with the same force. We are free to be who God says we are. No one and nothing else, including our own mistaken beliefs, holds sway.

We are princes and princesses of the Most High King. Because of what Christ did for us, we belong and hold esteemed value within our adopted identity. What others think, and even the mistakes we make, cannot change our identity in Christ or our standing with God.

As Chris continued to wrestle with God about his wife's health and his own developing relationship with God, his faith began to waver. He had come to God for greater peace, but everything had become worse. He was questioning himself and wondering how he was going to endure the stress.

Sandra was on a slow recovery, but Chris felt the pressure of providing for the family by himself if she was not able to go back to work. A hard worker, he couldn't seem to catch a break that would allow him to feel really successful. His business was fine, but the satisfaction wasn't there.

Again, he sought counsel from his pastor. Chris needed help as he felt on the verge of drowning. Bill challenged him to consider where he thought his identity came from, a new thought for Chris. As he reflected during the following week, he surmised that it likely came from his work and his ability to provide for and protect his family. Sandra's breakdown had rocked these key areas for him. He wasn't making enough to provide fully for them and he certainly hadn't been able to protect Sandra from this breakdown.

Bill recommended that Chris look at himself through God's eyes. He gave him a list of passages to meditate on and begin to internalize as his true identity in Christ. Chris wasn't sure how this would bring peace, but he was willing to try it.

Over the following weeks Chris diligently studied and meditated on the verses. He particularly focused on 2 Timothy 1:7, "I have not been given a spirit of fear but of power, love, and a sound mind"; on Hebrews 4:16. "I can find grace and mercy in time of need"; and on Philippians 4:13, "I can do all things through Christ who strengthens me."

He meditated on these verses during his morning study time as well as throughout the day whenever he felt stressed or overwhelmed. To his surprise, the more he did this, the more peace and courage he gained. Not only that, the passages seemed to regularly pop into his mind. While his circumstances were not changing, Chris was.

He even found he was more sensitive to Sandra when she was having a bad day. Because her well-being no longer affected his sense of identity and value, he became more open about extending the grace and mercy God was giving him, to Sandra.

He was surprised at what a difference this made. He was becoming the man and husband he wanted to be, and it was happening more as a pleasant side effect than by compulsion. In his quiet times he thanked God regularly for this unmerited gift.

Discussion Questions

1. As you read through Neil Anderson's list of I-statements based on biblical truths about you, do any stand out to you? Which ones resonate most? Which ones do you recognize may need more work to internalize and really believe?

2. If you came to *really* believe all of these statements, how do you think it could change how you interact with your world and the people around you?

15

Curious Case of a Calling

As we allow what we have realized about our unmerited identity to soak into our being, let's take steps to discover our purpose. Since God is the one who defines us and gives us our identity, likely He is the one to give us purpose. As we die to ourselves, which is ongoing in this life, we will discover new life rising out of the ashes; a life with hope and freedom that could not exist within our limited estimations. Adopting this renewed identity will include having a clear understanding of our purpose. So, let's explore what our culture and churches see as our direction and what God has in mind for us.

Our culture champions planning for the future and setting goals. We *must* find purpose and value in this life, and are taught that what we accomplish will provide that. Think of the people you esteem. Did they come to mind because of what they have accomplished or achieved? What standards do you use to measure your value in life?

What's more, sometimes our churches influence us with similar expectations. We are to strive to produce fruit and win souls to Christ. A well-lived Christian life seems to have its evidence in what we have *tangibly* accomplished for God. And yet, I wonder if this is really the focus we need to have. Instead of having to search for our purpose in what we accomplish, we can rest in the purpose that God has for us—our calling in life.

Before looking further at this purpose, let's clear up a major area of confusion about "calling" that trips up many of us. In his book *The Call: Finding and Fulfilling the Central Purpose of Your Life*, Os Guinness describes two distortions of calling we have and two separate types of calling we have.

The two distortions are considering our call or purpose in Christian life to be what is considered "full-time ministry" or to hold a segregated view of ministry and vocation. Both of these views, Guinness explains, fail to include our primary calling to be followers of Jesus. This brings us to the idea of two kinds of calling. Our primary calling is to be Jesus' followers and to live out every moment in response to Him. That is fundamental and for all Christians. Through this kind of focus, some may also receive a secondary calling. Vocationally, some Christians are called "to-the-ministry" as a secondary call and some to other types of work. Some Christians find a secondary calling in volunteering or serving in ways that have nothing to do with their vocation.

A secondary call, then, is something that some people receive in a direct or indirect way supernaturally from God. This can be in an immediate revelation or develop over time. However, God never gives us a calling for our own selfish indulgence. In fact, He gives it to us *for others*. Further, it is never separated from our original calling or at the exclusion of other aspects of life, which are lived out in conjunction with the secondary call.

Thus, if someone feels strongly that God has set them on a path of preaching, this does not excuse them from living and serving in other areas or roles in ways that bring glory to God. For instance, a preacher may also be a father/mother, husband/wife, brother/sister, friend, little league coach, and so on.

A secondary calling is not always someone's primary vocation, so some people work in one area to support themselves while fulfilling their calling. The Apostle Paul, for example, had to continue in his tent-making business to support himself because being a missionary to the Gentiles was not self-sustaining. In no way did this diminish his call or service to God.

Further, the perceived success of a secondary calling does not determine its value. The blog *God Reports* has told the story of Dr. William Leslie, a missionary in the early 1900s who thought himself a failure. After serving in a remote area in the Democratic Republic of the Congo (then the Belgian Congo) for seventeen years, he returned home believing he had failed to make any significant impact.

In 2010, a missionary group that went to the area realized that Dr. Leslie *had* made a significant impact. The group found a thriving community of reproducing churches in this area of the jungle. One church is a stone building holding 1000 seats and hosting people who walk for miles to attend services. Clearly, apparent evidence does not determine what will be a life well-lived for God.

Even so, many Christians have a mistaken belief that all Christians do, or should, have a secondary personal call in order to live a worthy or purposeful Christian life. This, too, is incorrect, and comes from the idea that purpose equates to this sense of individual calling.

God does not give secondary calls to everyone, and I do not believe we are intended to seek these out. Guinness intentionally identifies these callings as "secondary" because all personal calling must unequivocally be subordinate to our primary calling of living for and serving God in all things. In that perspective, it does not matter whether God reveals a secondary calling to us or not.

A secondary calling is not necessary for us to live as Christians. In fact, we are expected to and will be called on to give an account of what we did with what God gave us (1 Cor. 5:10), regardless of a secondary calling. He will examine how we lived our life in devotion to Him and how we allowed Him to move and bring glory to Himself through us. If our focus is on needing a secondary calling or on living for our own gratification, we miss the fullness of Him.

Of course, this will not affect our salvation or our entrance to heaven because those are based on having received unmerited favor from God. To be honest, I don't even think He will be angry with us. Instead, I think He will grieve *with* us when we realize the freedom, joy, and fullness we missed out on by seeking purposes or callings that were unnecessary or unsuitable for us.

Instead, when we live out our primary calling, when we are who He has created us to be by His definition and making, we experience a sense of blessing and joy that are better than the feeling of simply accomplishing something *for* God. Guinness puts it this way, "The truth is not that God is finding us a place for our gifts but that God has created us and our gifts for a place of his choosing—and we will only be ourselves when we are finally there." Because we have a clear call from God, we can live out our life for Him confident that He will be pleased. We do not have to search for something further. If He has a secondary call for us, He is big enough to get our attention and lead us there. For our part, the key is to live for Him—close to Him—and thus be able to recognize His leading.

Further, if we focus on our secondary calling and what we believe we must do before we die to fulfill what He has called us to, we will likely find setbacks extremely frustrating and discouraging. We may try to take control over our perceived calling and make it our own. All that we are, including our purpose and callings, are for and about God. He drives. He leads. He controls the results.

He also knows the number of days we have on earth. We do not even have control over that. He may have given us a calling knowing that we will not be the ones to complete it. Finishing up is never the point.

When we are holding too tightly to what we want to accomplish *for* God, even when He has pointed us in that direction and given us the passion to do it, we lose sight of our primary purpose

> "God has created us and our gifts for a place of his choosing—and we will only be ourselves when we are finally there." Os Guinness

and lose our freedom. Beyond that, we do not get to see the whole picture of our secondary callings. He unfolds them as He wills along the road. Rarely will He map them out in advance—another reason to live in daily dependence on Him.

I, for one, am thankful for that. I could not have handled all that has happened, had I known it in advance. I might not have followed any of my callings had I known what was coming. As it was, as I was finishing with one calling, God was preparing me for the next. In looking back, I am coming to see how they are connected into one calling, but He has still not revealed it in its entirety to me. I only get to see it in small steps.

Like walking through a thick fog and only seeing a set distance in advance, I know He sees where we are going but I am only permitted to see a few steps ahead. One major next step was God prompting me to earn my doctoral degree, only two years after I graduated from my master's degree. I fought Him. *Could He be serious?*

In all honesty, I had tried to figure God out and "play His game" to prevent this. How foolish, I know. I had sworn that I would never go back to school after I earned my first diploma, and God had "made" me get my masters. I resolved not to do that again, I would not say "never" to God and maybe He wouldn't ask me to.

You see, I had a mistaken belief that God intentionally asks us to do only what we don't want to do, just for that reason. I have heard others say this too. They fear fully surrendering to God in case He asks them to do things they don't want to do. For many, it is the fear of being sent into the mission field. As I think about it now, I am not sure why so many of us fear this.

Now, I don't believe that is His reason for asking us to do hard things, though I acknowledge it often feels that way. I also chuckle at thinking I could pull-one-over on God. As if He didn't know that I still didn't want to do it even though I wasn't going to say never! He is God, after all.

Well, after almost two years of wrestling and exploring and resisting, I knew there was no way around it. I couldn't give anyone a good reason for doing doctoral studies other than obedience to God. It was not going to provide me with a better job or more money. I was already in a role in which my salary was based on years of experience. Even so, the strong internal sense that I *had* to do this would not go away. Human logic was no help.

The only positive thing I could see, other than sheer obedience to God, was that I would likely gain confidence and competence in what I was doing. Thankfully, that happened. I truly believe I am a much better therapist because of what I learned and experienced. Others have confirmed this change. Unfortunately, I cannot say that I surrendered joyfully at any point through my six years of doctoral education. At each point where I had to pass a major test, I would honestly say to God, "if this is as far as we go with this, I am okay to stop." He never let me stop. So, I continued to trudge along.

The final stretch—my dissertation—took a year and a half to complete. I had no idea how to do original research, choose an appropriate therapeutic model (the kind of treatment used) for what I wanted to study, find the participants, do a qualitative study, or write a quality report. I pressed through, one step at a time. My dependence on God was so strong because I knew I was completely beyond my abilities and myself. He came through, but revealing only what I needed for each step—even when I lost 40 hours of work because my computer crashed.

Amazingly, I graduated. I now, almost exclusively, use the model I studied with the couples I counsel. As I knew from not being able to learn Hebrew for my master's degree, there are no guaranteed results. The guarantee is that He will lead and He will bring forth the results *He* desires. Our role is to follow and obey. Through surrendering my "need to know", I live freely, obediently, and joyfully.

When we can let go of needing to know or control what He has revealed, we are freer to move with Him when He redirects or changes our direction. We become flexible to His direction and more effective in His hands. We gain peace in trusting God.

Three months after her last day in her human resources manager position, Jennifer still had not found work. She was thankful that she had enough money to last almost six months, with careful spending. She was also thankful that she had wisely chosen to buy a house below her means. As she reflected, she realized this must have been God's guiding because her family had encouraged her to look for something "nicer."

This allowed Jen to take her time with the job search and divide her time into looking for work and spending deep reflective time with God. As a result, she slowly let her own dreams and aspirations go and became more open to what God wanted for her. She came to believe that, because God knew her better than she knew herself, and wants what is actually best for her, His plans would inevitably be better than her own. She still longed at times for a husband and a family, but had come to a place of wanting what God wanted *more* than what she wanted.

Jen's vocational focus had begun to shift as well. She was realizing that her value came from God and not from what she accomplished or what anyone else thought. While her family was pressuring her to find gainful employment, Jen was marveling at how relaxed she felt. She fully believed God had a plan for her, and her time was being well spent with Him instead of increasing her search for work.

As she prayed, she sensed God had something very different in store. As a result, she did broaden her job search to include mission agencies and ministry-focused organizations.

This would not please her family or provide the six-figure income she had been striving for. And yet, it seemed to offer more purpose and meaning. She wondered, "*Could God really be calling me to ministry?*"

While her family were all church-going Christians, they seemed to consider "full-time-ministry people" as *different*. Her family was comprised of "successful business people." They argued that Jen could make more money in business and so give more financially to ministry.

Even so, Jen grasped that she had to put her primary call ahead of achievement or pleasing anyone else—including herself. This allowed her to be open to becoming the HR manager at a fledgling Christian university in a fairly remote location. Their mission and vision captured her attention immediately. The position would not give her prestige or a high salary, but it felt right.

She felt as though God had been preparing her for this role all along. She could use her business acumen to help them become more professional and effective. Being single, she was free to start fresh in this developing university town. She could even rent her house, which would give her added income while she became more established.

Jen also was learning what it meant to struggle, persevere, and learn to surrender when things did not work out as planned. She was hopeful about her future for the first time in who knows how long. In fact, she felt that she was now starting to live her own life.

Discussion Questions

1. How would you describe a purposeful Christian life?

2. What do you think of us having a primary and secondary calling? Which, if either, has been your predominant focus?

3. What would it mean for you to let go of finding a secondary calling and putting more energy into your primary calling—to seek after God in everything you do?

16

A Prevailing Purpose

Now that we have discussed what our overarching purpose in life is—to know God and live in every way for Him—perhaps you're wondering how to live this out. Your critical voice (or "the critic" as I like to call it) will likely try to convince you that this goal is unrealistic or to dwell on just how unable you are to live this way. Rest easy. Accepting this calling is the first step. Fulfilling it is a journey toward becoming more and more like Christ. We will never fully arrive there this side of heaven. However, the more we live out our primary call, the richer our life will be.

We can shift the direction and intention of our hearts and lives to Jesus in the confidence that we can depend on Him. Remember, this is a partnership and we cannot live in obedience without the work of the Holy Spirit in us. Our part is the intention toward and dependence upon Him in all things. The Apostle Paul says that we are called to grow in maturity, knowing the primary calling that has been given to us by God. Then, Christ equips us and leads us to do the work He has prepared for us to do.

> [Christ equips] his people for works of service, so that the body of Christ may be built up until we all reach unity in the faith and in the knowledge of the Son of God and become mature, attaining to the whole measure of the fullness of Christ. Then we will no longer be infants, tossed back and forth by the waves, and blown here and there by every wind

of teaching and by the cunning and craftiness of people in their deceitful scheming (Ephesians 4:12–14).

When we move away from this overall purpose, we are not as satisfied or free as we could be. While we may find some satisfaction outside of living for God, life will not be as rich or fulfilling as God intends for us.

On some levels I think I would prefer if we could only find satisfaction in God. Wouldn't that make it easier to stay the course? However, He wants us to choose Him on an ongoing basis. When we do, our spirit will resonate with God's Spirit living within us and we will know greater peace, hope, and fulfillment.

I am still learning to live *more* freely and to surrender and die to more things. Just this past week, He revealed more of my stubbornness to me and convicted me of more that I needed to surrender. I had not realized how my resistance and begrudging obedience pained Him until then.

While I know obedience pleases Him, for most of this journey before I obeyed, I resisted. Eventually, I would recognize obedience as a good thing, as I grudgingly submitted. But, He wants joyful, whole-hearted obedience *even more*. He convicted me that it is not enough anymore to just obey.

For whatever reason, in His mercy, He knew that begrudging obedience was all I could handle until recently. This saddens me because I likely missed more fulfilling experiences throughout the years. It didn't have to be that difficult. It rarely has to be as difficult as we make it but we are limited by our humanness.

Please understand, when God convicts us, it is not to make us guilt-ridden. I do not feel *guilty* about my attitude. I feel sadness and genuine remorse because I grieved Him when I did not embrace what He was asking. He understood it and loves me anyway. Conviction is not His anger at work. Rather, it is His mercy. He is gently revealing an attitude (or behavior in some cases) that needs to change so that we can be more like Him, though I confess, at times He can be insistent. I want Him to delight in me, not to only love me through my brokenness.

The Holy Spirit enables me to go forward from that conviction with renewed determination and resolve to listen and obey more joyfully. I commit to not only obeying but embracing the tasks *He* has set out for me.

So, how do we live this practically? In *The Call*, Os Guinness suggests that our focus and attitude need to become increasingly directed toward an audience of One. In a world so focused on following others—church celebrities, business leaders, IT gurus, trendsetters—following God in that kind of way is challenging. To combat this, we must become aware of our need to bring God into every aspect of our lives and then regularly check ourselves and reorient when our focus is not on God. This is not a natural orientation, but with practice and repetition, our brains slowly learn to focus on God more automatically.

> While we may find some satisfaction outside of living for God, life will not be as rich or fulfilling as God intends for us.

One exercise I recommend for bringing God into your day is to set an alarm to remind you to focus on Him a few times during the day. It could remind you to pray or simply acknowledge God is with you and it is for Him that you are doing whatever you are doing.

Further, we are naturally inclined to seek the approval and appreciation of others, a real threat to obedience to God. Guinness says this is really where the problem of getting off track from our purpose lies. The real issue relates to whom we make our primary audience. If it is not God, we'll be sidetracked on our life's journey.

Others will approve of us or not, depending on their mood, bias, or even the rest of the crowd. If our focus is on pleasing them, we can be tossed back and forth. The Christian who is living in the fullness of Christ, as Paul described, is one whose focus is on God and is willing to stay the course for His approval, even when it is not in line with what others might think or say.

Even when the people we want to please are godly and well-meaning people, we will be distracted from the One who really matters. Their biases and interpretational filters can get in the way. If we instead make our audience God alone, we can consider guidance and wisdom from valued others, without needing to follow it simply because *they* think it's best. We evaluate the advice in order to discern how it fits with who God is and what He has been doing in our lives.

The better we know God, the easier we'll find it to obey; in fact, we'll *want* to please Him. The only way to get to know God well and what is pleasing to Him is by spending time with Him and by being in His word. Both maturity and being able to follow God closely come through time spent reading and studying the Bible as well as having real conversations with Him (as opposed to rote, disconnected prayer).

In *100 Days in the Secret Place*, compiled by Gene Edwards, Madam Guyon, a seventeenth-century mystic suggests "praying the Scriptures" as a way to draw closer to God. This is not study; it is more devotional in nature. The process is to choose a short practical passage and read it slowly, focusing on the words and being open to what God might be saying to you through them. You are not interpreting the passage; you are using it more as a grounding point to connect with and listen to God through quiet reflection.

We can protect ourselves by remembering that God cannot contradict Himself. Thus, if we feel that God is asking something contradictory to His Word or character, it is not Him we're hearing. However, if we sincerely seek Him, and genuinely want what He wants, we will be able to receive direction from Him. He is *able* to reveal anything to us regardless of us, but He prefers to work with open and willing hearts. Always check what you sense or hear against His Word and character. Then, when you find what you sense to be God's leading to be consistent with who He is, you can safely go forward, knowing you are focused in the right direction.

In addition, it's good to watch for confirmation of His leading or new guidance as you journey with Him. Confirmation often comes in repetition of the message through different means. You may sense something from a passage of Scripture and then you hear a preacher saying something similar. At another time, you may feel the message is coming to you through songs or through conversations although you did not bring up the topic.

As well as working one-on-one with us, God shapes us through our life with others. God is relational and puts us in relationships to make us more like Himself. In making us in His image, He intended us to value relationships highly. Marriage, children, friendships, work relationships—all relationships are about learning to interact the way Jesus does in loving, healthy, boundaried, generous ways. To be a safe person and not self-seeking.

It is in the difficult moments in relationships where we have opportunities to learn these healthy ways of interacting. Trials in relationships draw us into deeper dependence on God. With Him we have the resources and strength to deal with our jealousy, envy, frustrations, and our desire to control someone else. When others do not or cannot meet our needs, we can take comfort in God to do so.

In this journey we may need to revisit our view of dependence. While our culture considers dependence on anyone other than self as weakness, in His Kingdom, dependence on God is considered a profound strength. Fulfilling our primary calling involves becoming more dependent on God in every moment and understanding our connection to Him. When Paul speaks of Christ as the head of the body in Ephesians 4:15, he is making a comparison to the various parts of our body and its systems depending on the human head for direction. So too, we are to depend on Christ, our head, to direct us.

Does this mean we are not to use our own minds? Certainly not! God gave us the ability to reason and make choices on purpose. The key to this partnership is to intentionally direct our minds to depend on Him, to have His filters as ours. In general, our well-being depends on our ability to intentionally regulate our thoughts and emotions.

We are meant to actively tune in to our thinking processes as well as our responses to the thoughts that pop into our minds. We have been given the capacity to use our logic and accomplish great things. At the same time, fulfilling our primary calling involves training our minds to focus on and think with God's perspective.

With God as our focus and primary audience, we are free to release all to Him. As we grow into deep dependence on Him, we no longer need to control where we are going or how we will get there because we know Him well enough to trust Him with the results, wherever He leads us.

When dealing with difficult people, we ask God to help us respond in a way that pleases Him. When faced with situations that we do not know how to navigate, we ask Him for guidance and wisdom, trusting that He is with us. For instance, when trying to manage exhausted, cranky, uncooperative children at the end of a harrowing day, we cry out to God to give us patience, wisdom, and kindness so that we can get them to bed without adding to the frustration. In all things, He is our refuge and strength, an ever-present help (Psalm 46:1).

Even when doing things we are good at, we still ask God to be part of it and lead us so that He receives glory in it all.

Amanda continued to seek after God with renewed passion as she grieved her mother. After being able to depend on Him when her old boyfriend tried to reconnect, she knew He would be a resource for her whenever she needed Him—as long as she surrendered and turned to Him.

She also realized that, while it had never seemed doable before, as she depended more on Him instead of her own strength, she could allow Him to help her. She accepted that while He wasn't going to simply make life all better, He would walk through the valleys with her. She was not alone. She allowed that realization to sink in and radiate warmth. Knowing she had a companion in God felt like receiving a needed hug—oh, how she longed for her mother's hug!

Friends started noticing that she was changing. While she was still Amanda, she seemed to have more focus and purpose. She still enjoyed hanging out, but her conversations seemed to steer back to God more often.

As she reflected on her education and her future, she allowed herself to admit that teaching would not likely be an option anytime soon. However, because her mom and dad had been financially responsible with insurance, there was money for her to pay off her school loans and then travel, something she had always wanted to do but had dismissed because she couldn't afford it.

She pondered and prayed about where God might be leading her. In the past she had always kept God on the periphery. Now, she wanted His guiding for each step of the road. Amanda sensed her travels could be more purposeful than simply sight-seeing. As she prayed, the idea of short-term missions came to mind. It was not something she had ever wanted to do, but now the thought was not as scary, after all, she was only thinking about short-term.

The next Sunday she was surprised to realize that they were having a missionary guest speaker at church. Her curiosity stirred and with it a sense of excitement ignited. After the service she found out from the speaker that a school was being opened in the village where she served. The missionary said they were looking for someone willing to help start it up.

Amanda was shocked. It was not a permanent position, but they were expecting it could be a six- to twelve-month assignment with potential for more. She let the missionary know she would be praying about this and would get back to her. Amanda left a little in awe.

The village was in a Spanish-speaking community and Amanda was thankful for her decision to continue with her Spanish throughout school. If she did go, she would not need to go through language training. She would need other training to prepare to go but that was doable. She had the time.

She was not sure where that might lead, but the more she considered it, the more right it felt. This would be consistent with His character and His Word, and was consistent with what God seemed to be doing in her life. Her education would not be wasted if she went this route, even for just the year.

For the first time in her life Amanda felt she was living in God's will for her. She was making Him her number one priority and it didn't matter where that led her—she was going with Him.

While the grief and pain of losing her mom remained strong, she also took comfort in knowing her mom would be proud of the person she was becoming. She could imagine her mom up in heaven smiling and cheering her on. Amanda knew she was going to make it through.

Discussion Questions

1. What areas of your life have you invited God into? When do you depend on Him; is it even in the areas you are good at? How do you think things would change if you invited Him into all areas of your life?

2. What would it be like to be free of having to control results and where your life was taking you? Does that sound freeing or terrifying? Take time to wrestle with God about this. Ask Him to reveal His loving plan for you. Remember, He may not reveal a secondary plan at this time. Are you open to living out a more focused primary calling?

3. When you are following God's leading, what is your attitude? Is it begrudging, joyful or a mix? Could God be asking you to surrender more in this area?

17 | Letting Go of What's Lost

As we continue our climb out of this valley, the air is fresher. The sun shines brighter. We feel refreshed and exhilarated. As we look back, even the past is taking on a new perspective.

We are closer to moving forward and embracing our freedom, with our new understanding of our identity, new purpose, and clearer focus. But let's take time for a deeper look at what it means to die to ourselves and how God enables us to overcome the pain of our crosses. I have found that understanding all aspects of what God was asking of me helped me embrace dying to self. My hope is that this will take you to a deeper understanding and encourage you to grab hold of this counter-cultural experience.

In the middle of the Gospel of Mark, Jesus talked to His followers about the importance of being willing to deny ourselves, even to the point of dying, in order to fully live as His disciples.

> Then he called the crowd to him along with his disciples and said: "Whoever wants to be my disciple must deny themselves and take up their cross and follow me. For whoever wants to save their life will lose it, but whoever loses their life for me and for the gospel will save it. What good is it for someone to gain the whole world, yet forfeit their soul? Or what can anyone give in exchange for their soul?" (Mark 8:34–37)

For a long time I didn't understand what Jesus was talking about in saying that if we wanted a close relationship with Him, we would have to give up our very life. It sounded so dire. Did Jesus really want me to find some way to lose my life physically or was He using this language because of the cultural climate? Certainly, in the first few centuries after He died many people were martyred. While I do not believe He was suggesting we need to seek out martyrdom, it seemed He was asking a whole lot. For many, following Him like that seems unattainable. After all, we are ordinary people.

And yet, He was talking to ordinary people who would have to make choices to follow Him instead of taking the easy or expected way, just like us. For them, the choices to follow Him often had more dire consequences that could include rejection, exclusion from family and communities, or even death. Still, He told them that following Him would bring real life while protecting themselves from discomfort or even severe suffering would lead to spiritual death.

Then I realized that He makes a way. If He wants this kind of devotion, *He* will draw it from us. We only have to *be open* to Him and depend on Him. Often the first steps are asking God to make us want this and to remind us to refocus our attention on Him. When trials come, you then ask God to show you how He might use these difficulties to draw you closer to Him. Also, ask for His perspective to replace your own interpretation of the situation.

Let's explore what Jesus meant when He said we have to deny ourselves and take up our crosses and follow Him. Denying ourselves is another way of talking about shifting our allegiance to God alone instead of living for our own purpose and gain. *All of life is to be about Him*, not us. That phrase always gets me. As I reflect on it, I feel the burden of having to have things my way lift. When it is all about Him, I can let go and allow Him to direct my path. He knows better where we are going. Not some things, not just the spiritual things, *all of life*. In everything, we deny ourselves for the sake of Someone far greater.

So what does Jesus mean by denying ourselves? It means considering Him and His priorities above our own. In Mark

10:17–23, a rich man asks Jesus how to inherit eternal life. Though his question appears to be about salvation, in reality, he's looking to achieve perfection. This is the reason for Jesus' response about following the law. The man says he has done all of these things. But Jesus knows he is not truly seeking after God and points to the one thing that this man is holding between himself and true surrender to God—his wealth. Jesus tells him he must sell all he has and follow Him. The man leaves discouraged because he knows he is not willing to do this.

This passage is not prescriptive, but it is a warning and teaching for us. The way to handle money or our attitudes about it, can get between us and God. Do you give to God and the needs of others as a first priority or out of what is left over? Our culture pushes us to have more. Denying ourselves could be choosing to buy a house below our means so we always have extra to give away. Or, it could mean choosing to have less and live on one income so one spouse can take care of the kids at home, ensuring that they are taught the ways of God and Christian values by you. Another path of denial would be turning down a job that requires you to be dishonest or unethical even though it could make you a lot of money. It could mean doing the right thing in a situation when you know that decision will cost you heavily.

How we spend our time can be something else to consider. We might be asked to spend time serving when we would rather be doing something for ourselves.

There are many ways to discern the areas we need to give over to God. The key is evaluating your priorities and asking God to search you and know your ways (Ps. 139:23–24) so He can convict you and change your ways to be more in line with His. Regularly praying through the end of Psalm 139 is a great way to invite God to change you and surprise you with more insights.

Taking up our crosses is similar to denying ourselves. Like Jesus, when people were crucified they often had to carry their own crosses to the site where they would be hung. When Jesus talked about taking up our crosses in surrender to Him, it meant being willing to suffer injustice for His sake. This doesn't mean never fighting for justice, but simply being willing to suffer accepting that we may not be treated fairly. So often I hear clients say, "It's not fair." Most times I fully agree. And yet, we have the opportunity as Christians to respond differently than the world does. We can respond with grace and kindness even when it is not deserved. We can be willing to go the extra mile without complaint or grumbling.

The key with taking up our crosses is going through things without grumbling or needing others to see the injustices. Instead, we can pray and choose to trust that God sees them and will bring justice in His timing and His way, rewarding us later for our attitudes and responses. He empowers us to go through the adversities. This attitude is not weakness or an admission that we do not deserve justice; quite the opposite. It is laying down our rights *by choice* to honor the One who laid down His life for us.

Then Jesus goes further in describing the depth of commitment needed to be a disciple: those who want to save their lives will lose it and those who are willing to lose their lives will gain it. *What is this about?* This passage has two levels of application, one in relation to life with God in heaven and one to the way we live as disciples now. In the original context, Jesus knew that soon after His death Christians would regularly be asked to deny their faith or face persecution, and likely, martyrdom. Even in His own time, people often had to pay a price for being close to Him. Ultimately, we all are given the choice to follow Jesus or walk away—none will escape this. Gaining life on earth to live as we want is life without Jesus and results in loss of eternal life with Him.

However, this passage has a deeper meaning for the believer: a life of devotion to Christ and of really *living* will involve greater and greater denial, and in fact, death to self. Jesus made that requirement abundantly clear. And when we let go, He replaces our old nature with new life that far surpasses the struggles and pain of our old self-focused ways. Conversely, when we insist on having our rights and desires met, we are constantly frustrated and discouraged when they are not. When we no longer need to have things our way, we are more able to flex and move with the challenges with ease and peace, without seeing them as inconveniences.

If we accept His salvation and we live only minimally for Him, unwilling to surrender all and follow His plan and purpose, we will never fully experience what God has for us. We may know some peace and hope for the future and at times we may feel Him close to us. Yet we will not have the freedom of knowing we are fully taken care of no matter what happens in the content of life. When challenges come or injustices are made against us, we will tend to be pulled into them and need to fight or prove ourselves. Peace will evade us.

Conversely, those willing to let Him transform them have both eternal life *and* abundant life in the now. Then when life throws trials and injustice at us, we may be briefly knocked off balance, but we will be able to stand firm again rather quickly. The intensity of life experiences diminishes because we trust in the goodness of God.

Knowing that He is good and everything that happens to us passes through Him first, allows us to trust that He will give us everything we need to get through a bad time. We accept that He wants us to get through it and that He will use it to mature us. This brings peace and a release from needing to strive, defend, or figure all of life out. We trust that, when things are wrongly taken from us, God has a plan for us and we will not be overcome by the loss. We can rest in knowing He is still in control.

In my first career, my boss would assign projects to me and then reassign them to a co-worker who would get all the credit for my work. It was unfair and unjust. I think she also got higher raises than I did as a result. One day I called my father to vent in frustration. He validated the injustice of it and then refocused me on God. He asked whether in the end, when all is said and done, in light of God, would any of that matter? I admitted no. He advised me to do what is being asked as though I was doing it for God and to release the results to Him. It

> Those willing to let Him transform them have both eternal life *and* abundant life in the now.

made a difference. The injustice continued but my focus shifted to God and I wanted Him to be pleased with my responses more than to have my boss respect my rights.

I remember a novel in which a Christian would always say "God is good" whenever bad things happened, her way or reminding herself of His goodness instead of succumbing to fear or distress. We can do this also. When hard things come, remind yourself, God is good. He will see me through this. He has a plan in this even if I don't see it. This will enable you to move forward and deny your self-interest, or carry your cross, or simply carry on, with a renewed sense of peace.

As Linda and John continued to navigate the changes in their relationship, Linda felt increasingly agitated. She knew John was praying for her and that his faith had grown to the point that he was drawing near to a decision. He wasn't nasty or condemning about the distance between their outlooks. He was loving, and she could see it pained him to be pulling away.

Then, one Saturday after returning from a long walk alone, he asked her if they could talk. With tears in his eyes, John painfully let Linda know he was moving out to take some time to figure things out. He asked her to consider God in a new way. He said that, though he loved her deeply and did not want to add to her pain, he had to become clear about where God was leading him before he could continue with her. God had to be first for him.

She knew he would not be back if she didn't return to God. He might not come back anyway. She also knew, too well, that just going through the motions would not be enough. It had to be real.

This thrust Linda into a full-on-battle with God. She had spent most of her life running from Him and swearing she had no use for Him. To add to her pain, her mom and her partner kept finding joy and freedom in their lives—which they fully attributed to God alone.

What she was seeing in them was not what she had experienced with God or church years ago. *Who is this God? And why didn't He care about her like that? Why does He keep letting her go through pain in her relationships?* The thoughts surprised her. *When had she started to view her life through what God allowed and didn't allow?* She did not want to need anyone!

And yet, she felt a longing for more than she had, not just for John. While she hated to admit it, she wanted the peace and confidence that her loved ones had. She wanted to feel good enough too.

The difficult separation from John gave Linda time to continue her battle with God. She also risked talking more with her mom. Each time she would start with, "This doesn't mean anything—I don't want to be pressured. I just want to ask a few more questions."

Helen answered her questions without pushing her daughter, and on occasion offered to pray with Linda. At first Linda said no, but slowly she started to be open to it—as long as her mom didn't pray outright for her to return to God. Helen complied, knowing full well she was praying fervently for Linda in her private prayers.

After a few more months of questioning, wrestling, and anguish, Linda had had enough. She was alone, distraught most of the time, and not happy with her life. She decided to risk letting God have it all. *Her way clearly wasn't working!*

So, Linda knelt. While she knew that wasn't necessary, for her, this was the posture of surrender. She had to die to everything she had been about for almost 35 years. She had to be willing to let God change all of her.

She prayed, "Okay, God, I'm done. I can't keep running and I can't keep fighting you. I believe you want me back and I now know you want all of me." She repented of taking her life into her own hands and defiantly rejecting Him. Knowing her old ways had to die to allow God to give her this new life, she asked for forgiveness, and she asked for what the others had. What she had growing up wasn't enough. She implored, *God please show up this time.* She couldn't do it without a sign He was real.

The thought came to her: "Are you really ready to give me everything? Even if John never returns?" She thought about that. *Everything.* She returned to praying, "Yes God, I am willing to give you everything if only you will give me what mom and John have, even if he never returns." As she prayed that, knowing that for the first time in her life she really meant it, peace filled her. The weight of her life seemed to lift, and she knew something had changed.

Linda also knew that, to keep her peace and hope, she had to follow through on her commitment. She had to give God everything. For her, that meant finding a Bible so she could really know Him. She didn't know how to live in surrender, but she would depend on Him to show her. That's what mom had said. "Jesus will show you, baby step by baby step."

Discussion Questions

1. As you look at your life freshly, in what areas do you feel God may be asking you to deny yourself? What do you see that you haven't submitted to God so you can experience the freedom we have been discussing?

2. What are you still clinging to that God is prompting you to let go of? (If anything keeps coming to mind, take time to prayerfully look at it. God often speaks to us through repeatedly bringing things to mind.)

18

Less of Me – More of You

We are almost at the top of the other side of the valley now. Though the climb will still challenge us at times, I hope you are now enjoying the benefits of the dying to self process with God—that you are sensing God taking more and more control over your thinking and perspectives. Without us even realizing it, He puts the desires in our hearts that He plans to work out in our lives. He leads and guides us rather than us needing to figure out where we are going. In fact, He becomes greater within us, and who we figured we were, naturally, becomes less. In this way, life begins to work more smoothly. Let's explore this concept further.

If we live surrendered and with God's perspective, we will thrive and live with fluidity and peace in spite of our circumstances. When we tap into His perspective and trust that He is good and has good plans for us, we can experience the content of life differently. That is the hidden gem that many people miss! Abundant life—in God's definition rather than ours—can be lived regardless of circumstances under the sun.

We were created to surrender to God and rely on Him in all things. It is never about us. Even in our churches this is sometimes not a clear focus. Letting God determine our identity, our purpose, and our route to achieve whatever He has for us is the only way to function in our original, intended form.

In a very self-sufficient society, living our lives depending on God is challenging. Even so, as we live out dependence, we will realize that we have access to God's resources and are freed from having to depend on our limited selves. The tyranny of "shoulds" is lifted. We rest in knowing He has the plan, and He will work it out in us as we depend on Him and let Him transform us.

The final death is of our perspective on our purpose and future plans. We do not get to choose our primary purpose or how it plays out. That has already been established and we will not *fully live* our life unless we are surrendered to His plans for us.

John the Baptist is an example of someone who knew who he was and what his role was and lived accordingly. He was not puffed up about how God was using him to impact the multitudes. When Jesus came to the Jordan, John was not upset by Jesus' growing popularity. John knew his identity, his value and his worth, and his purpose. In fact, we read in John 3:27–30 that he told his disciples,

> A person can receive only what is given them from heaven. You yourselves can testify that I said, 'I am not the Messiah but am sent ahead of him.' The bride belongs to the bridegroom. The friend who attends the bridegroom waits and listens for him, and is full of joy when he hears the bridegroom's voice. That joy is mine, and it is now complete. He must become greater; I must become less.

John knew Jesus had to increase in influence and his role had to decrease. John was the forerunner to Jesus and now that Jesus had come on the scene, John's purpose had been completed. Taking this language and making it personal, as the Holy Spirit resides within us, Jesus' influence must become greater in our lives and ours must become less.

To help us understand our role, God uses container imagery in Scripture. He says we were created to be vessels for Him. We are His temple. He lives *in* us and He is able to direct our paths and see us through anything. Paradoxically, as we give over control of ourselves and allow the Holy Spirit to fully inhabit and possess us, we become more of who we were created to be—more of Him working in us and less of us needing to drive our lives.

When we were first married, my husband and I were not making a lot of money. He had recently finished his degree and hadn't yet found work in his field and I was working in my old career not sure how to make the transition to counseling. I was not happy with my job and not doing well at it. I could do project management but was not as skilled at managing the people who worked under me. I knew God had led me to be a therapist, but quitting a job that had consistent pay for something that I had to build seemed unsafe. My husband is not a risk taker. This put me in a challenging position because I strongly believed God wanted me to make the transition but my husband could not see how that would work financially.

I prayed that God would make a way. He did, but not the way either of us would have wanted. First, I was demoted and then learned the company planned to cut my salary significantly. My boss was sending me a clear message that the company was not happy with my performance. This was my second experience with facing profound failure. Even so, God reminded me that my identity is not in my performance and I sensed this was the closing of that old career.

The pay cut was the push we needed to risk having me start as a full-time professional psychotherapist. I started with four clients. That is *not* enough to pay bills with, let me tell you. That put a strain on our marriage in those early months, but still I released my trust to God and begged Him to work this out. During that time, He taught us to trust Him with our finances and within a fairly short period, He blew us away with His provision.

Throughout this and other experiences, God has taught me to trust Him more and rely on Him fully. The results are not my own. The ways I think my life should play out are not necessarily His plans for me. I must decrease, He must increase.

Sometimes I am blown away with His extravagance, other times I am forced to dig into Him because He is not doing things the way I want them. Through it all, my identity comes from Him alone and I can have peace regardless of what life throws at me. Success or failure, He is still God and I am always His. He is growing me and refining me through it all.

> If we live surrendered and with God's perspective, we will thrive and live with fluidity and peace in spite of our circumstances.

We are the clay, He is the potter (Jeremiah 18:6). He is good and has good plans for us. Even in trials and challenges when we are dependent on Him and trust that nothing is beyond Him, we can rest knowing He will see us through whatever it is for His glory and our righteousness. The goal in life is Him and becoming like Him—more of Him, less of me. More of Him, less of me. The more we invite this, the freer and more peace-filled we become. Even when the world is in chaos, we do not have to be.

We have choices within the purpose God has set out. Living out our purpose in the ways God has designed us to be is not confining, but rather freeing. As a result of dying to self in greater and greater measure, we live the life we were created to live!

Again, this is not so much about the content of life, which is fallen and broken. This is about transcending the content even when it does not change or improve. The power in this message is that we are able to be really okay and live in this freedom, even if nothing in our circumstances changes. What power does the enemy or anyone have against this kind of internal peace and assurance? Nothing can shake this once we really grasp it.

As crazy as it sounds, I now find the idea of dying to self and being less of me and more of Him exciting. Take this passage from Oswald Chambers' *My Utmost for His Highest*,

> [God's] call has nothing to do with personal sanctification, but with being made broken bread and poured-out wine. God can never make us wine if we object to the fingers He uses to crush us with. If God would only use His own fingers, and make me broken bread and poured-out wine in a special way! But when He uses someone whom we dislike, or

some set of circumstances to which we said we would never submit, and makes those the crushers, we object. We must never choose the scene of our own martyrdom. If ever we are going to be made into wine, we will have to be crushed; you cannot drink grapes. Grapes become wine only when they have been squeezed.

When I read devotionals or hear messages like this, my spirit cries out "yes"! This is an unnatural response but when God has been at work in your life for a while, and you have learned the pure joy of being transformed by Him, you too will want to let Him do whatever He needs to make you more like Jesus.

As the months wore on, Sandra began to recover from her burn-out. Chris was so thankful for God's mercy in healing her. Through counseling she had gained perspective and was able to set better boundaries and was more effective with self-care. However, she remained uninterested in God or going to church.

Chris knew if he pressed the issue it would, once again, become a sore spot for them. At the same time, he was not willing to not have God in his own life. He had come too far and knew God too well now.

Unfortunately, Sandra became more and more antagonistic toward Chris because he would not let this "whim" go. Chris worked hard to not react badly at the sarcasm and jabs in Sandra's retorts, when he told her he was going to study group or church. Regularly, Chris prayed for patience and gentleness with her.

No matter what he did, it seemed Sandra was becoming increasingly selfish rather than emotionally healthier. She would threaten that since he had something so important that it pulled him away from the family, she would find hobbies and he wouldn't be allowed to comment on them.

Her hobbies included going out drinking and dancing with friends and leaving Chris to watch the kids. She claimed this was part of her self-care. He knew that her counselor had not recommended it, but she had stopped going to the counselor as well.

Chris had hoped that what his pastor and study group said about Sandra turning to God through this trial would be true. But life with Sandra grew harder. Chris was left wrestling with God again over his wife and marriage.

During one of his prayer times, Chris felt like God was asking him if he would pull away from Him because of the situation with Sandra. Chris said that he would never allow that. Then it seemed God was asking him to stay the course; to keep loving her and praying for her even as she became colder and more defiant. He felt God would use this to deepen his dependence on Him and to bring Himself glory.

Chris didn't like the sound of this. He would have to let his biggest hope and dream die for that to happen. He realized he was fully expecting God to make his marriage better, yet it seemed God was saying "no" and requiring more of Chris instead. The only way he could endure Sandra's growing antagonism was with God's strength and wisdom.

He surrendered Sandra and his hope for a happy and healthy marriage to God afresh. Even if she never came to the Lord and remained distant and cold, he would love her sacrificially. If she wanted to leave, that would be a different conversation, but he committed to stay and be the husband God was asking him to be, regardless of his wife. *"More of you God, less of me,"* he prayed.

The road was hard, but along the way he realized God was fully with him. His primary purpose was clear. His value and worth were secure, regardless of his wife's rejection. He committed to love God and be conformed to His image no matter what—and it was happening!

He would be a light in his home, even if his family was not interested in seeing it. He would accept their ridicule and coldness so that one day, he could receive his "well done good and faithful servant" from the One who loved him most.

While some days were harder than others, Chris felt more alive and cared for by God than he ever had before. Chris continued to live out his daily life and marveled at how God allowed his journey of greater dependence on Him to affect the lives of others outside his family. Chris never dishonored his wife in what he shared with others. Most people had no idea how challenging his marriage had become. The amazing thing was, people seemed to seek him out for guidance and wisdom—wisdom He knew was not his own. He had a calm and joy that surpassed what most people experienced. The journey was day-to-day at times, but Chris wouldn't trade the closeness he found with God in for anything.

Discussion Questions

1. Read 1 Corinthians chapter 3. Consider what Paul is saying in light of what you have been learning and reading here. How does this passage bring together the ideas of dying to self, allowing God to lead and have control, Him getting the glory, and us gaining freedom and reward when we allow this?

2. What would it mean to you if you focused less on yourself and let God's influence and control became greater in your life? Can you see any freedom that could come from this?

19 | Freedom to Be Who I Am Intended to Be

We have made it to the top of the other side of the valley. Let's take in the incredible vista. There is hope, joy, and unimaginable freedom on this side! As you have been discovering, letting go of our need to be in control frees us to have more joy, be more patient, show more love and compassion, and be better able to forgive readily. We are more stable and filled with peace even when unbelievable challenges come our way. In fact, we can "Consider it pure joy, my brothers and sisters, whenever [we] face trials of many kinds, because [we] know that the testing of [our] faith produces perseverance. Let perseverance finish its work so that you may be mature and complete, not lacking anything" (James 1:2–4). We can begin each day open to God's leading and accepting of whatever comes.

As we have learned, this surrendering and dying to self is not a one time exercise, but a series of surrenders as God reveals new areas of resistance. Some come with changes in age and stage of life. Others He reveals only when we are ready to deal with them. We cannot rush that process or determine which things He will address when. We have the rest of our lives.

As you may have discovered, the first few times you surrender are very painful, but as you become more accustomed to the working of the Holy Spirit you will sense more quickly when He is at work (though you may not always know what He is doing at first).

Even so, you will lean into and pray for God to quickly put to death whatever it is, because you will have complete faith that the other side will be better! Knowledge is not enough to follow though; the final dying is only possible when God empowers us to let go.

A few years ago I was wrestling with some selfishness, though I cannot recall what. I imagine it was to do with having my way about something I knew He did not want for me. I do recall an entire summer of praying "God, please let me die to this thing so that I can be past the anguish of it." I knew I needed a perspective change but I couldn't make that internal change myself. Finally, something in me shifted and I felt released from my resistance. What a relief.

While we cannot control the dying itself, what we can do is seek and ask for Him to do whatever He needs to do to make us like Him and to use us to bring glory to His name. In praying that scary prayer, know that He will begin to bring new things to your attention that you will be asked to die to. Do not be discouraged, or think something's gone terribly wrong. This opportunity is a good thing.

We can also prepare ourselves and stay grounded by seeking more of Him through spiritual disciplines. There are many, and different ones will be easier and harder for different people. Richard Foster, in *Celebration of Discipline: The Path to Spiritual Growth*, describes and gives instruction on how to practice twelve different types, including Christian meditation, prayer, fasting, solitude, simplicity, worship, and confession.

As we learn to spend time with God and sacrifice ourselves for Him through these disciplines and others such as giving and thanksgiving, we learn to sense His presence more frequently. Thanksgiving is a wonderful spiritual discipline that psychology has recently recognized as a powerful exercise in experiencing well-being. Research shows that something shifts in our brains when we are thankful. I believe that when we are thanking God directly and are in relationship with Him, even more blessing results. (As an aside: I love it when research confirms what we have always known from Scripture!)

Being thankful changed my view of God and allowed me to realize just how involved in my life He really is. It also enabled me to receive little "hugs" from Him, which I cherish. One happened while I was doing my master's degree. It was a late class and that night my professor had lead us through a healing prayer exercise where we went back into a painful memory and then invited Jesus into it. The experience itself was very healing for me.

Then as I walked out of the school, I was oddly alone, and I saw the aurora borealis in the shape of a white dove. I had never seen the aurora as it is not common in my area. I stood in awe as it moved and shifted from the dove shape. As it changed, other students came out and were blessed by the light. I received that dove shape as a gift specifically for me, particularly in light of the healing He had just given me in my class. Perhaps others in the neighborhood had seen it, but in my mind this was a wonderful hug from God.

Other "hugs" can be seeing a deer in the distance as you are walking or driving, seeing rainbows, sunsets and sunrises, whales or dolphins jumping unexpectedly, hearing a kind word when you really need it, the perfect song coming on the radio, traffic opening up when you are running late, anything really. So often we take these little blessings for granted but when we are intentionally thankful for them, we learn to see God in everything and we are doubly blessed by them. As we practice thankfulness and the other disciplines that draw us closer to God, we find it easier to surrender to Him.

After surrendering, you will find yourself much better equipped to handle difficulties and deep disappointments. Yes, God still allows painful things to happen—that is one way in which He matures our character. Now though, when troubles threaten to undermine us, we are in a better position to pause and remember that we have given Him permission to be in control and the freedom to work in us however He sees fit. We can assure ourselves, with confidence, that we will still be okay. The assurance is in knowing He is still good and cannot not be good, and He is always with us.

Even when we're at the end of ourselves, when we have no idea where to go or how we will survive, we can turn to what we know—that He will carry us through. This idea of being carried comes through in Mary Stevenson's poem, *Footprints in the Sand*. It's a story of a woman who dreamed that her life was captured in footprints in the sand. There were always two sets, representing her own and Jesus', but in times when she went through suffering and trials, there was only one set. When she asked the Lord about this, He told her that it in those times He had carried her.

This poem reveals what we often experience. In times of suffering and trials, we do not always feel His presence. But we can have comfort because we know Him well enough to trust that He is always with us, no matter what we feel. He will see us through to the other side of the pain. We will likely still feel the natural emotions of the suffering. That is not a lack of faith; it is part of the process. Emotions are always allowed. He understands our pain, and He has felt our pain.

The key to understanding and responding well to our emotions is to allow them space and to walk through them, all the while, not letting them determine our truth. Jesus was in deep anguish the night before His crucifixion and He felt pain and even severe anxiety. We know this because Dr. Luke wrote that Jesus sweat blood (now understood as a medical condition called hematidrosis: the mixing of blood with sweat due to severe anxiety or stress) as He implored the Father to remove the cup (His impending crucifixion and punishment for all of humanity's sin) from Him (Luke 22:44).

Experiencing stress, anxiety, grief, or pain is not sinful or wrong. Jesus never sinned but He did experience anguish to the extreme. Passages like John 11:35 illustrate His grief when a dear

> After surrendering, you will find yourself much better equipped to handle difficulties and deep disappointments.

friend died. At the same time, as seen in His prayers before His crucifixion, He did not allow His feelings, as intense as they were, to deter Him from the Father's will. We may feel many things, but we can remain devoted and surrendered to Him and His will, even when it hurts to do so.

At other times, after sensing God's closeness and leading, we'll go through periods when we do not feel Him at all. He seems to suddenly disappear. We cannot hear Him, sense Him, or feel Him. Even reading the Bible seems flat. Prayer seems to bounce off the ceiling instead of reaching Him. Such times have been called the dark night of the soul and are experienced by many Christians. Some suggest that all Christians experience times of spiritual dryness. These periods, though desolate, are not a punishment or a sign of a weakened faith. In fact, God intentionally withdraws the *sense* of His presence for our growth.

He chooses not to reveal Himself in order to draw us closer to Him. His hope is that we will continue to seek Him on deeper levels—like tree roots stretching deeper through dry soil to find water. We commit with our will to believe what we know about Him, even when our senses betray this knowledge. As we stay faithful, our confidence and trust in Him unexpectedly deepen. Our dependence shifts even more to Him alone, and away from our need to *experience* Him.

Even those who have known God for years can question whether He exists or is real. Some people feel faith is on the line and may walk away from God and Christianity. Michael Molinos says in *100 Days in the Secret Place*, "In such times you are either going to leave off prayer, and perhaps even a large part of your Christian walk, *or* you will be driven to a comfort which has nothing to do with the outward senses."

Most, however, who go through this come to realize the reassuring truth that their faith and understanding of God will not let them turn away to anything else. There really is nothing else or no one better. That is the struggle. In the dark night of the soul one feels lost and disconnected but nothing else seems to provide a better answer.

In time, His time, we will release more of ourselves and what we thought we understood, and again become aware of His presence. As we do, we will find that God's faithfulness is even more enduring and our journey with Him feels more secure. We emerge knowing that God is faithful both when we experience Him and when we do not. This deeper knowing creates an unshakable security and trust in Him.

If we enter another dark night, we will know that nothing can remove us from His hand (John 10:28–29). The dark night of the soul is an invitation to go deeper, not a risk of falling away—though it often feels that way.

We will have to wrestle with problems (financial issues, work problems, family disputes, loneliness, physical ailments or mental disorders, and the like), but "if God is for us, who can be against us?" (Romans 8:31). Remember, this verse is talking about our security, not our experience on earth. Heaven and eternal hope are secure. The worst that can happen to us here is death—resulting in immediately being in God's presence in heaven and having freedom from all suffering.

Molinos goes on to say that as a result of persevering in these dry spells:

> You will learn the gift of perseverance, which has many fruits and advantages. You will develop a weariness toward the things of this world little by little, and by slow degrees, the desires of your past life lose their strength; new ones toward your Lord arise.

God does a deeper work within us during these times. Temptations become less potent and we find our interests being redirected to things that are pleasing to God. Even things that are not particularly sinful or wrong, but are just not useful or helpful in drawing us closer to God change. I know for me, my taste in music has changed more than once over the years. I have become more aware of the content of songs and how a great many direct us to sinful actions or attitudes. Songs I used to believe were harmless and fun, no longer hold the same appeal. In honesty, I have come to enjoy silence far more than any music. It has never been a strong pathway for me to connect with God. While I fully enjoy songs of worship, I have found silence and solitude, particularly in nature, to be much stronger pathways of worship for me. Each person is different in this regard and God works with our personalities and preferences to draw us deeper into Him.

With this freedom, God can be our focus. We will find it easier to let life relate to Him and to live out our focus within the content of our days. He will be at the forefront of our minds and our responses to ordinary things will be filtered through our relationship with God and what He is doing in our lives. That doesn't mean we'll be so "heavenly minded, we're no earthly good." No, we'll pay even closer attention to what is happening and participate in it more fully, but with His values. We will invite Him to be in the middle of it *all*.

You may face the temptation to shift your focus to the byproducts of life in Jesus. However, joy, peace, and freedom can never be the goal. If we make them our end, we will miss them. When Peter was walking on the water toward Jesus and saw the storm, he took his eyes off Jesus and began to sink (Matthew 14:28–31). The freedom and excitement of walking on the water slipped away. Keeping our eyes on Jesus and focusing all that we do toward Him—our main audience—results in freedom to do far more than would be humanly possible.

When we let Jesus be our goal and focus, we experience unexplainable joy and surpassing peace, along with freedom and lightness. Further, we gain the wisdom to see and understand things from His perspective. We may not be permitted to see everything, but we become keenly aware that there *is* a perspective at work that is higher and more accurate than our own.

We begin to notice the fruit of the Spirit being exhibited in our lives without our effort. At first it's surprising and awe inspiring. *How did I do that?* The growth feels good and natural instead of stressful and pressured. Prayer and reading the Bible can also become easier. Striving is no longer a concern; only freedom and joyful dependence remain.

As James continued to battle his post-treatment Lyme disease, he recognized his need for God even more. The months wore on and his commitment to not let the disease defeat him strengthened. At the same time, he realized that fighting it was a losing battle that only brought greater frustration. He needed to accept his reality and learn to make accommodations.

When he could not get out of bed, he dug deeply into his Bible, and his prayer life increased significantly. He often had days when his body was too tired or sore to move much. As a result, he got into a routine of spending large amounts of time with God almost every day. Dependence became a need instead of an uncomfortable "should."

Throughout this journey he felt God's closeness in ways he had never imagined possible. Scripture jumped off the pages and new insights came with it. Up to now, James had insisted on being in control, but now He was tasting the sweetness of God's love, even when he felt out of control. He didn't like the pain and exhaustion, but the peace and joy within his times with God were deeply restorative.

His wife noticed differences. She marveled with him about how he was softening and gaining wisdom and influence. Because he had to be cautious about his use of time, James had become intentional with it. His family and the people at church were amazed that this busy, driven man was becoming a man of patience and wisdom. He would often be invited to sit and listen to others and then could provide encouragement from what he had been studying.

At home, he and Barb started reading the Bible and praying together each morning. When he was able, they would sit on their back deck and enjoy the birds singing from the ravine behind their house. When he was not well, she would bring coffee into the bedroom and they would read in bed. Both of them came to love this time, which could sometimes last a couple of hours. Their relationship deepened.

James learned how to conserve his energy to some degree. When he wanted to attend events outside the house that were important to him, he would rest so it was more likely he could attend. When he had energy, he battled with himself not to expend it quickly because that could wipe him out for many days.

Even so, James continued to release more of his desire to have the life he had wanted and to embrace and seek out the beauty and value in his new life. It was certainly not what he might have chosen, humanly speaking. And yet, as time went on and his relationships with God and Barb continued to deepen, he found himself becoming more thankful for this rude interruption.

As he reflected, he knew that without this illness, he would never have slowed down enough to recognize his need for God. He would have continued to perform and do things for God without tasting the riches of depending on Him daily. He would have judged his worth and value in what he accomplished instead of in what he now realized was God's view of his identity.

While physical weakness still frustrated him, the freedom of allowing God to order His days made them much easier to handle. James could never commit to anything with certainty. He had to take each day as it came. To deal with that, James released everything to God and came to trust that God would set up his appointments and give him the energy to keep the ones He wanted him to keep. When James had nothing to give, he rested assured. At the same time, he truly enjoyed his times with God.

Complete surrender definitely had benefits that James could never have understood before. This disease had not conquered him—it had freed him! Only God could make that possible.

From our vantage point at the top of the other side of the valley, what beauty do you see? Can you taste the freedom available to you? Let's see what it can look like for others …

Discussion Questions

1. What problems, challenges, and suffering are you dealing with? How could you surrender them to God and allow Him to meet you in them freshly? How could His perspective change your experience of these things even without changing their content?

2. When have you been in a dark night of the soul? What questions did you ask? As you reflect, what do you think God was asking you to let go of and die to? Consider how you can lean into God more, wrestle with Him, and pour out all of your feelings and fears to Him openly. He wants to take you deeper.

3. If you have taken steps to surrender to God, how is life different? Who do you think you will become?

20

A New Reality

I want to encourage you with more examples of how adopting God's perspective on change can apply to very difficult life circumstances. I confess that in the short space of this chapter, I cannot do these examples justice. Please understand if you are going through any of these situations, I am not trying to be trite in offering a high-level description of dealing with your pain. I understand it is real and not easy to overcome. Yet, if you are willing to press into Jesus and wrestle with God, I believe you can overcome challenges like these and any others you are facing.

Adopting God's Perspective

19 and pregnant

When we're nineteen, we never expect to become pregnant. As a Christian, this can be especially shaming. Yet, often in our teens and early twenties, we feel almost invincible. We recognize that difficult situations can happen but we never expect them to happen to us. If you are a Christian, pregnancy is not God's way of punishing you for having sex before marriage. It is simply a result of engaging in sex, regardless of precautions taken. It can be terrifying because it thrusts you into having to make decisions about your life that you are not ready to make.

Remember, God knew what was going on before this happened and allowed it for a purpose. He loves you. He loves this baby. He has plans to use this to draw you closer to Him through it. He may even use this little person to bring profound changes and growth in your life and the lives of others.

Yes, you have to face the comments and possible disappointment or even the rejection of others. This does not define you. Now you can choose to turn the "disgrace" into a positive. Turn to God and surrender to Him once again. You will have days when this seems impossible and the enormity of the future is daunting. Even so, day by day and moment by moment, seek His wisdom and allow Him to unfold His plan for you and this child. You won't be told how it will play out. This will require stepping out in faith and choosing to believe He is good and He loves you very, very much.

If you chose to end the pregnancy, you know a different kind of pain. God knew that was going to happen too. Do not run from Him; He still loves you. Seek Him, His forgiveness, and His healing. Even this He can somehow use for good. It is a long journey but He wants to draw you closer and heal your pain, regret, loss, and more for you. This, too, does not define you.

2 weeks from the wedding and your fiancé calls it off

After all the planning and anticipation, your fiancé says the wedding is off. Of course, you are devastated, shocked, hurt, embarrassed, angry, or perhaps relieved, depending on the situation. You have so many things to sort out. What do you do about the plans, the bookings? How do you let people know there's no wedding? The finances? The honeymoon is booked and paid for. Everything is paid for! People have bought tickets to travel to be with you. You may feel shame or fear of abandonment or that you'll never marry.

Perhaps you called off the marriage, knowing the relationship could not work for the long haul. In that case, you may feel regret, sadness, and possibly compassion and pain for your ex. This was not how you wanted your relationship to go but you simply cannot go through with the marriage, knowing it will not work out. You may feel relief in making the decision but that doesn't lessen the weight of it. You anticipate rejection and being shunned and hope that some people will understand and support you. It's scary to take this kind of step and you likely wrestled with it a long time before having the courage to call it off.

Either way, these feelings could overwhelm you. If, however, you can step back and take God's perspective, you'll find it much easier to work through your distress and the reactions of family and friends. With His perspective, you will realize that when one of you thinks the relationship is not going to work, sooner *is* the time to end it. Marriage is wonderful and difficult, but "until-death-do-us-part" is a long time.

You might doubt your value or ability to make good decisions when it comes to romantic relationships. You may question if you will ever find the right person to marry. You may also be angry at God, wondering why He allowed the relationship to get this far. You may also want to jump into another relationship to alleviate the pain or prove to yourself that you are still desirable.

Now is the time to pause and do some soul-searching—a bit at a time, if necessary. Discover who you really are. Ask yourself what drew you to this person. What went wrong? Ask God to reveal anything in you that needs healing or change in light of the break-up. Ask where else He might be leading you. Remember that you are cherished by Him and He is with you. If this relationship has ended, it is likely God is protecting you from something worse.

At the same time, do not avoid the pain with self-medication, denial, or overcompensation. Take time with the healing. Be where you are, and know, God will not leave you in a broken place forever. Lean in and allow God to use it to heal you, grow you, and draw you into Himself even more. He will see you through and honor the time you take with this process.

Being caught in a pornography addiction by your wife

Hiding away at your computer in the basement, you didn't hear her come home and down the stairs. You have been battling an addiction to pornography throughout your marriage and once again you had told yourself this was the last time. Then you looked up and saw the anguish and devastation on your wife's face. Shame, horror, and defensiveness flooded you. "This is not what it looks like," you say. "It's nothing. I can stop. It has nothing to do with you." Nothing makes the situation better.

After the argument finishes and she walks away, you are left to try to figure out what to do. You do not want this to be a part of your life. You have an inner knowing that watching porn is not healthy for you, and yet, when life becomes stressful it is the release you return to. And then you face shame and frustration again.

You have asked God to take it but for some reason He hasn't. Now your wife knows and you fear consequences or exposure. What will she do? Who will she tell? How can you go forward if someone else finds out? At the same time, you may be feeling a strange sense of relief. It's out now. You have to do something about it.

I know this is scary and you feel extremely vulnerable. At the same time, help is available to you. You cannot tackle this addiction on your own, or even just with God. He allowed your wife to find out as a means of pushing you to face the problem in a way you haven't been willing to up until now. He knows the pain it causes and He wants to free you from feeling you have to give in to this temptation.

Help can include going to see a therapist, talking to your pastor (although not all pastors are well equipped to address this), or finding a support group like Celebrate Recovery or XXXChurch. com which has groups of other men facing the same struggles. If the first person you do talk to dismisses it or minimizes your addiction, seek help with someone else. It may feel good to hear it isn't really a problem but inside, you know it is and real help is available.

Know that God sees you and loves you very much. He knows how hard this battle is and what it will take for you to finally put it to death. You may have to relinquish it repeatedly, as you learn to depend on Him for comfort rather than this form of self-medication. The road will be long and often up hill, but you will find hope and freedom as you face and accept the reality of this addiction and learn to use tools to make different choices.

Accident and injured

A screech of brakes, an airbag inflates, and you find yourself being taken to the hospital in an ambulance. But you were just returning home on a usually quiet country road. You know you're not in good shape, what with all the tubes and bruises. Surely, you'll recover soon. But you won't. You learn that you need a serious operation, that you've lost part of a limb, or it is unlikely you will ever walk again.

Your life has been turned upside down. You can't take that dream vacation. You won't be playing sports again. Or perhaps you now have to re-learn or rely on others for ordinary things you took for granted. Be gentle with yourself. It's okay to grieve and be angry.

In time, allow God to give you new hope. God has not forgotten you. He is not punishing you or being cruel. He loves you dearly. He knows—He knows. He has plans to bring good from this. Remember, He defines good, and sometimes it is painfully hard to see the good in your hurt. Lean into Him. Allow Him to be your comfort. You'll know when it's time to let go of what your life was and accept that it will never be the same or as you anticipated. Wrestle through the dying of everything you once knew for as long as it takes. Then, let God write a new story for you.

God will not abandon you or put you out to pasture. He will create a new path with new dreams. Don't give up life. Work for the recovery you can have. If dependence on others has become a new reality, try not to fight it. You can also depend on God to give you a new identity. Joy can come once again.

Diagnosis of a terminal disease

You hear the dreaded news that the test results are not good, that the treatments are no longer working. Hearing that death is closer than you anticipated is devastating. After all, you have fought for your recovery, and now you are faced with the news that nothing more can be done. It is natural and important to grieve what will not be. That is part of the process; God understands that completely.

If you are comfortable wrestling with God and surrendering your life and concerns to Him, you'll be able to refute any suggestions that He has abandoned you or your family. You'll look for the opportunity to draw ever-so-much closer to Him. In light of the brevity of time, you'll realize even more often that things that once seemed so important, no longer matter in the same way. You can ask Him to help you release what you used to value.

Spend more time with God to gain His peace and perspective. You may not have the strength to read your Bible, but perhaps someone can read to you or you can listen to music or on-line sermons. Even if you cannot find the words or strength to pray, know that the Holy Spirit lives inside of you and prays on your behalf as you focus on Him.

For Christians, death holds hope as well as loss. For us, heaven is not merely a nice idea, but a real place with God; it's a new adventure. You may not think so at first, but as you allow God to draw you near to Him, He will give you that comfort and hope.

Your loved ones can also be transformed by the closeness of God during this journey. Take time for the important things and ask God to protect you and your loved ones from anger and bitterness. Feeling anger at times is natural. The key is to not let yourself settle there. Surrender all to God in this and He will bring hope and deep comfort. He is enough.

Your spouse has checked out of the marriage

They say marriage is supposed to be happily ever after. Well, at least until one of you dies. You never expected your spouse to check out. For some, this involves staying legally married but mentally and emotionally checked out. That's not what you expected. It is painful to live with someone who is disinterested and uncaring.

This does not mean *you* need to check out as well. Here is where perspective can help. When all of life is about God and becoming more like Him, you can be assured that He has allowed this for that purpose.

Instead of focusing on what your spouse is not doing and how they are not meeting your needs, return your focus to God. Lament to Him, of course. Pray for your spouse to change; bless your spouse in God's name. Then, surrender them to God and ask Him to change *you*. Ask Him to help you to be the best spouse you can be even when yours is not changing. Do this for *His* "well done good and faithful servant."

God sees your heart and your efforts. Know that as you love this person who is being unlovable much of the time, you are investing in rewards you will abundantly receive in heaven. God will honor you for your efforts. He will change you into someone of great character and Christlikeness through the process. God can be the spouse yours is not, until God sees fit to make changes—or even until the end of time.

Some of you are protesting because the sexual side of your relationship is missing, and God is not able to meet *that* need for you. Even so, He can help you endure that loss. You will not suffer harm by not having that part of your life. It is painful and difficult, but we can endure many types of suffering if we depend on God. When the longings reappear, run to Jesus and surrender them again.

God can see you through this and you can be happy in your marriage, even though you are not in a healthy marriage. Your spouse is not responsible for your happiness and well-being. That is between you and God, and He can use this to bring greater wholeness and joy, even if nothing changes.

Your grown child has walked away from the Lord to live in sin and rebellion

When the child you raised, who's doing so well in many areas, walks away from God, your heart breaks. You do not have any control over the situation. Even though you love them and have done your best to raise them to know God, things can cause them to turn away. You may have contributed to some of the reasons and contributed nothing to others. Nonetheless, you could not have stopped this from happening, no matter what you tried. Their faith is a product of God, their own choices based on the free will that God gives all of us, and your witness during parenting. You are only one element in the equation.

The tendency is to blame yourself or search the past for what you could have done differently. This is futile and destructive; we cannot undo or redo any moment of time. God did not set life up that way. We are limited.

So now you are facing the painful reality of what *is* and that you are powerless to change your child's life. At most, you can have influence, but even that may be limited when they are grown and living in rebellion. They likely do not want to listen.

As with any loss, take time to feel the pain and grief of what could have been—what should have been. Wrestle with God about the promises you believed He gave you for your children and how you raised them. Then, slowly, painfully, surrender your children to God. He gave them free will and this life is now theirs to live. You cannot live it for them, though you only want what is best.

When God allows painful things, He doesn't waste them; He uses each one in the lives of those who seek Him. Ask for His comfort. Seek His perspective and be willing to release the future if He does not give you the answer or full picture you want. Keep steady by remembering that He is good. He loves you deeply and He loves your child even more than you do. Truly.

Pray that God would send people to your child who they will listen to and who will speak truth to them. Continue to pray for their surrender to the Lord. Trust God's timing and goodness. Even if you do not live to see change in your child's life, know that God will see you through the pain of that loss. As you surrender control to Him, you can transcend even this. Until you do, the loss will threaten to overcome you. Baby steps in all of this. God will lead you, if you want Him to.

One Last Affirmation

Surrender and dying to self gets easier the more we let go. The experience of God's goodness and grace, even when our circumstances do not change, increases the more we practice this discipline. He is worth it. Being open to seeing things the way God sees them, even when nothing in the situation changes, changes us and allows us to experience the situation with more hope, peace, and perspective. Be gentle with yourself in this.

Our journey may lead us through the wilderness or deepest valleys—*but*—we can take courage in knowing that God has allowed us to face it and that we are never alone. He knows the way out, and He will use the journey for good. We can trust that He is at work, bringing good from all things for those who seek Him. When it feels like it is too much, simply stop and in that moment know that He is God and He is supporting you.

Nothing can steal the deep peace and comfort of knowing that we are not alone and someone good and loving is in control. God usually won't rescue us *from* the turmoil, but He will use all of it to mold and mature us. Amazingly, life takes on a richness and fullness that is not possible when we are limited to our own perspectives. Recognizing God's hand and purpose in everything is both comforting and awe inspiring. He will blow us away repeatedly! And in the end, He will reward us abundantly for a life surrendered to Him.

Acknowledgments

When God first put it on my heart to write this book, I was hesitant. Once again He was asking me to move way out of my comfort zone into an area where I had no idea where to even begin. I am very thankful for Kim G., Leanne, and Dayna who chatted with me that late night at a women's retreat and encouraged me to take this step. That talk was the turning point in my taking this journey into the unknown.

I am also thankful to Kary Oberbrunner and the AAE tribe for their direction and encouragement along the way. Without that, I do not know that this could have been accomplished.

To my editor, Krysia Lear, I am so very thankful for your patience in guiding me through this process. I had no idea how hard this would be but you were always gracious and I am thrilled with what we have been able to put together through this process.

Then to my friends and family who have been incredible cheerleaders, encouragers, and editors. Thank you Gerry and Sheila (dad and mum), Julie, Jessica, Ian, Kim D., Rachel, Lise, Gary, Denise, Merry, Leanne, Lynn, and Hannah, who are always there to pray and encourage me. And a special thanks to Vince, my husband, for your willingness to have me embark on this crazy journey without knowing where it might lead. You all have been amazing and have kept me going in this crazy adventure. Thank you.

Endnotes

1. Kimball, Dan. 2003. *The emerging church: vintage Christianity for new generations*. Grand Rapids, Mich: Zondervan.

2. Pettegrew, Hal. "Perspectives on the Spiritual Development of the Aging Boomers." *Christian Education Journal* 5, no. 2 (2008): 305.

3. Brown, Bettina Lankard. "New Learning Strategies for Generation X. ERIC Digest No. 184." (1997).

4. Armour, Stephanie. "Generation Y: They've arrived at work with a new attitude." *USA Today* 6 (2005): 2005.

5. Black, Alison. 2010. "Gen Y: Who They Are and How They Learn." *Educational Horizons* 88 (2). [Sage Publications, Ltd., Phi Delta Kappa International]: p. 94. http://www.jstor.org/stable/42923795.

6. Kimball, Dan. 2003. The emerging church: vintage Christianity for new generations.

7. Cavey, Bruxy. 2007. *The end of religion: encountering the subversive spirituality of Jesus*. Colorado Springs, Colo: NavPress. p. 37.

8. Wright, J. Stafford. 1994. *Zondervan NIV Bible commentary*. In Barker, Kenneth L., and John R. Kohlenberger (Eds), Grand Rapids, Mich: Zondervan Pub. House.

9. Erickson, Millard J. 1998. *Christian theology*. Grand Rapids, Mich: Baker Book House.

10. Erickson, Millard J. 1998. *Christian theology*.

11. Williams, J. Mark G., Danny Penman, and Jon Kabat-Zinn. 2012. *Mindfulness: an eight-week plan for finding peace in a frantic world*. Emmaus, PA: Rodale Books.

Bibliography

Anderson, Neil T. *Victory Over the Darkness: Realize the Power of Your Identity in Christ*. Minneapolis, MN: Bethany House, 2014.

Boa, Kenneth. *Conformed to His Image: Biblical and Practical Approaches to Spiritual Formation*. Grand Rapids, MI: Zondervan, 2001.

Cavey, Bruxy. *The End of Religion: Encountering the Subversive Spirituality of Jesus*. Colorado Springs, CO: NavPress, 2007.

Chambers, Oswald. *My Utmost for His Highest: The Classic Daily Devotional*. Uhrichsville, OH: Barbour Books, 2015.

Edwards, Gene. *100 Days in the Secret Place*. Shippensburg, PA: Destiny Image, 2001.

Foster, Richard J. *Celebration of Discipline: The Oath to Spiritual Growth*. San Francisco: Harper & Row, 1998.

Guinness, Os. *The Call: Finding and Fulfilling the Central Purpose of Your Life*. Nashville. TN: Word Publishing, 1998.

Lewis, C. S. *Mere Christianity: A Revised and Amplified Edition, with a New Introduction, of the Three books, Broadcast Talks, Christian Behaviour, and Beyond Personality*, Edited by Wayne Martindale and Jerry Root. New York: HarperSanFrancisco, 2001.

_____ *Screwtape Letters with Screwtape Proposes a Toast: Revised Edition*. New York: MacMillan Publishing Company, 1982.

McGee, Robert S. *The Search for Significance*. Houston, TX: Rapha Pub, 1990.

Willard, Dallas. *The Divine Conspiracy: Rediscovering Our Hidden Life in God*. San Francisco: Harper San Francisco, 1998.

Young, William P. *The Shack: Where Tragedy Confronts Eternity*. Newbury Park, CA: Windblown Media, 2007.

Additional Recommended Reading

Anderson, Neil T. *Bondage Breaker*. Eugene, OR: Harvest House Publishers, 2006.

Crabb, Larry. *Finding God*. Grand Rapids, MI: Zondervan, 1993.

Postema, Don. *Space for God: Study and Practice of Spirituality and Prayer*. Grand Rapids, MI: Faith Alive Christian Resources, 1997.

Smalley, Gary. *Your Relationship with God*. Carol Stream, Ill: Tyndale House Publishers, 2006.

Thomas, Gary. *Authentic Faith: The Power of a Fire-Tested Life:* Grand Rapids, MI: Zondervan, 2002.

_____ *Thirsting for God*. Eugene, OR: Harvest House Publishers, 2011.

About the Author

Tara Lalonde is a registered psychotherapist in Ontario, author, and speaker who has been helping people find life transforming change for over a decade. During that time she has grown to love working with people who are looking for deeper and more profound journeys with God. She has a Masters of Divinity from Tyndale Seminary and a PhD in Professional Counseling from Liberty University, which allow her to not only address therapeutic issues, but also equip her with a keen understanding of how the Christian faith integrates with and infiltrates all of our lives.

In her counseling practice she focuses on treating individual adults and couples dealing with issues such as anxiety, depression, burn-out, emotional issues, women's issues, marriage, self-esteem, forgiveness, communication, family/identity issues, OCD, and Christian spiritual growth.

Tara strives to live what she teaches and this can be seen in her authenticity and lack of pretense in all that she does. Most of all, Tara has a passion to see people free to live and enjoy how God truly created them.

To follow Tara and her ministry, check out her website at taralalonde.com.

The purpose of my instruction is that all believers would be filled with love that comes from a pure heart, a clear conscience, and a genuine faith.

1 Timothy 1:5

Made in the USA
Charleston, SC
22 December 2016